A BIRD'S EYE VIEW OF LIBRARY AND INFORMATION SCIENCE (LIS) EDUCATION, RESEARCH AND TRAINING IN INDIA

A BIRD'S EYE VIEW OF LIBRARY AND INFORMATION SCIENCE (LIS) EDUCATION, RESEARCH AND TRAINING IN INDIA

Prof. A. A. N. RAJU
Formerly Head
Dept. of Library & Information Science
Osmania University
Hyderabad – 500 007

Ess Ess Publications
New Delhi

A BIRD'S EYE VIEW OF LIBRARY AND INFORMATION SCIENCE (LIS) EDUCATION, RESEARCH AND TRAINING IN INDIA

ISBN: 978-81-7000-729-6

₹ 1100/-

First Published 2014

Published by:
Ess Ess Publications
4831/24, Ansari Road,
Darya Ganj,
New Delhi-110 002.
INDIA
Phones: 23260807, 41563444
Fax: 41563334
E-mail: info@essessreference.com
www.essessreference.com

Cover Design by *Patch Creative Unit*

Printed and bound in India at Salasar Imaging Systems.

Dedicated to the sacred memory of

DR. S. R.RANGANATHAN

(1892-1972)

Father of Indian Librarianship

and

Library and Information Science Education

Contents

PREFACE

Library and Information Science (LIS) Education in the Country has a history of a Century. During these hundred years it saw several ups and downs and slowly emerged as one of the important professional courses to train the required manpower to manage various types of libraries and information centres in the country and elsewhere.

It is being offered in about hundred LIS Departments of Universities and other institutions including Open and Distance Learning Universities and Institutions in the Country. At the University level Courses in LIS such as BLISc, MLISc, MLISc (2-years) and Research Courses like M.Phil and Ph.D. is being offered. The Open and Distance Learning Universities / Institutions have enabled more people to pursue these Courses in a large scale. At the semi-professional level National and State Library Associations have been offering Certificate (CLSc) Courses.

To meet the ever changing needs of LICs and to keep track of latest developments in the field, especially, the advent of Information and Communication Technologies (ICT), the Curriculum of LIS Courses are being updated. UGC has appointed a number of Committees to look into Curriculum of LIS

Courses and suggest the necessary modifications keeping in view the latest developments. The recommendations of these Committees not only deal with Curriculum aspects but also infrastructure facilities, staff strength, computer laboratory, working hours, staff-student ratio and related aspects.

Thanks to Dr. S. R. Ranganathan's dynamic leadership and initiative, LIS education in the Country travelled a long way. His reports on University and College Libraries and LIS Education form the basis for growth and development of LIS education in the Country. He is truly regarded as the Father of Indian Librarianship and LIS Education in the Country. His seminal contributions in the form of books, articles, state of the art reports have greatly contributed to lay strong foundations for LIS Education in the Country.

Several books have been published on various facets of LIS education in the Country. In addition, several International, National, Regional and Local Conferences, Seminars and Symposia have been organized especially from 1960s. The National and State level Professional Associations such as ILA, IASLIC, IATLIS, APLA, BLA, DLA and MALA have contributed to the growth of LIS Education in the Country. Proceedings of some of these Conferences have been published enriching the literature on LIS education in the Country. The professional journals also have published and are publishing a number of articles on various aspects of LIS education in the Country. These sources form the basis for writing the story of LIS education in the Country.

The present book *"A Bird's Eye-view of LIS Education, Research and Training in India"* is another latest addition to the existing literature on LIS education in the Country. The ten Chapters in the book deal with: 1) LIS Education, 2) Contribution of Library

Associations, 3) LIS Education in the Universities, 4) LIS Education through distance mode, 5) Committees on Curriculum Development, 6) Professionals Associations supporting the cause of LIS education, 7) LIS Research in India, 8) Ph.D. output in LIS Departments, 9) Training of LIS Professionals and 10) Future of LIS Education, Research and Training in India. These ten chapters throw fairly bright light on state of LIS Education in the Country. Especially Chapter 8) Ph.D. output in LIS Departments is highlight of this book which provides information about the yearly award of Ph.Ds including the first research scholar to obtain Ph.D. from the Department and number of Ph.Ds produced by each Research Supervisor / Guide of a particular Department. In all forty LIS Departments have been covered in this Chapter. Rarely such information is available from already published books on LIS Education in India.

Concerted and sincere efforts have been made to collect as much information as possible from LIS Departments in the Country. Some have responded positively and immediately and provided the required information. But majority of the LIS Departments turned a deaf ear to my repeated requests over phone and through e-mail. This was the reason to cover only forty LIS Departments in the Country in Chapter 8.

It is fervently believed that the present and latest volume on LIS education, research and training in India will meet the needs of LIS professionals, teachers of LIS and Research scholars in the Country and elsewhere. The Chapter-10 "Future of LIS Education, Research and Training in India" is another important and useful Chapter presented in the book.

— **Prof. A. A. N. Raju**

ACKNOWLEDGEMENTS

Several Professional Colleagues have helped me to collect relevant information for writing this Book. I sincerely believe that but for their unstinted cooperation, it would not have been possible for me to write some of the Chapters in this Book, especially for gathering information on Ph.D. output in LIS Departments (Chapter-8).

I would be failing in my duty if I don't mention the instant support and cooperation received from *Prof. C. R. Karisiddappa, Prof. R. S. R. Varalakshmi, Prof. N. R. Satyanarayana, Prof. V. Vishwa Mohan, Prof. D. Chandran, Dr. Pushpanjali Jena, Prof. A. A. Vaishnav, Prof. Narendra Lahkar, Prof. Subal Chandra Biswas, Prof. Ranjana Vohra, Prof. A. Amudavalli, Prof. . V. Malhan, Prof. M. Nagarajan and Dr. Bulu Maharana* who in spite of their busy time schedule helped me to get the required information and I am thankful to all these Professional Colleagues.

Especially I must record my sincere appreciation of the help and support I could receive from Prof. C. R.Karisiddappa who strived very hard to get information on Ph.D. output of the LIS Departments from the States of Karnataka, Kerala and Maharashtra.

I would also like to thank Dr. A. R. Chakravarthy, Asst. Professor, Osmania University Library, Hyderabad and Dr. P. Mallikarjuna Rao, Documentation Officer, P. S. Telugu University, Hyderabad, who constantly helped me to get relevant information from the maze of information sources available in these two University Libraries.

Sri Sumit Sethi, the young and dynamic Chief Executive M/s Ess Ess Publications, New Delhi, came forward whole heartedly to bring out this publication and I am thankful to him.

Lastly, but not the least, I would like to thank Sri M. Madhusudan, my close friend for the past four decades who prepared typed copy of this publication.

—Prof. A. A. N. Raju

1

L.I.S. EDUCATION

1.1. HIGHER EDUCATION SCENARIO

"Education is the kindling of a flame not the filling of a vessel". **—Socratees**

"The highest education is that which does not merely give us information but makes our life in harmony with all existence". **—Rabindranath Tagore**

"Education made us what we are".

— C.A.Helvetus

Education has been defined by the O.E.D. as "the systematic instruction, or training given to the young in preparation for the working of life, by extension, similar instruction or training obtained in adult age. Also, the whole course of scholastic which a person has received. Often with limiting words denoting the nature or predominant subject of the nature or predominant subject of the instruction or kinds of life for which it prepares, as classical, legal, medical, technical, commercial, art education"[1].

According to Wikipedia "Education in its general sense is a form of learning in which the knowledge, skills and habits of a group of people are transferred from one generation to the next through teaching, training or research. Education frequently takes place under the guidance of others, but may also be autodidactic (a self taught person). Any experience that has for motive affect on the way one thinks, feels or acts may be considered education"[2].

Higher education is generally referred to as education imparted in the universities and colleges which include teaching research and social services activities which include both the undergraduate and post-graduate levels. University system constitutes both constituent and affiliated colleges. In India most of universities and colleges including PG Colleges come under Central / State governments. After liberalization, many private universities have come in to being offering varied courses at UG and PG levels including doctoral research programmes.

At the time of independence, the country had just 20 universities and 500 colleges. The number of universities and university level institutions had increased from 30 in 1950-51 to 634 in 2011. At present there are 43 central universities, 297 state universities, 100 private universities, 129 deemed universities, 651 Institutions of national importance and other university level institutions established under various state legislations. The number of colleges also increased manifold with just 695 in 1950-51 to 33,023 by 2011. Today, India has largest system of higher education in the world in terms of number of institutions i.e. 634 universities and 33,023 colleges and emerged as the third largest in terms of enrollment in the world[3].

There is no acceptable and comprehensive definition for LIS education. The glossaries and dictionaries on LIS defined the two terms i.e. 'Library

Science' and 'Information Science' separately, and definition for the compound word 'library and information' is not available. Therefore one has to improvise definition or explanation for the compound word Library and Information Science. LIS education may be explained, if not defined, as the systematic, instruction of "Professional Knowledge and skill with which recorded information is selected, acquired, organized, stored, maintained, retrieved and disseminated" and also "management of information in all its forms, including channels (formal and informal) and technology used in its communication". This explanation is based on the definition of 'Library Science' and 'Information Science' found in Online Dictionary for Library and Information Science by J.M. Reitz[4].

LIS education in the country took roots at the beginning of the 20th century. It has just history of 100 years when compound with other disciplines in the social sciences. It is younger and had its teething troubles before consolidating itself in the 1960s. At present in about hundred library schools of universities offer courses at different levels offering degrees such as: BLIS / MLISc / MLISc (2-Years), M.Phil and Ph.D. This is in addition to semi-professional level courses being offered by Library Associations at the national and state levels.

The genesis, development and spread of LIS education is briefly presented in the succeeding pages.

1.2. McFARLANE TRAINING PROGRAMME: THE BEGINNING

LIS education in the Country has completed 100 years in 2011. It has a century of chequered history. To begin with, informal training programme was launched by John McFarlane, the then first Librarian of the Imperial Library, Calcutta (now the National Library, Kolkata) to train the personnel working in the library. The formal training took place during 1903 and 1906. Later, the programme was extended to the professionals working in Calcutta[5]. The year 1903 should have been considered as an important year for the genesis of LIS education in the country in an informal way. But most of the authors on historical development of LIS education in the Country took the year 1911 as the beginning where classes were started, in the formal sense, to impart professional training for the personnel working in the public libraries of the erstwhile Baroda State.

1.3. BARODA LIBRARY SCHOOL

The Baroda State has a rich tradition of public library movement and the credit goes to Maharaja Sayaji Rao Gaekward III who initiated public library development in his State as early as in 1910. He appointed W. A. Borden (1854-1931) an expert from USA to plan free public library network to render free public library services to his people. Borden went to Baroda and initiated to work of developing public libraries in the State. Borden was appointed as Director of the State Department of Libraries, Baroda in 1910. This proved as an act of great wisdom in fact, lay the real foundation of modern library movement in this country. Newton M. Dutt observed that "during his three year's tenure of office Mr. Borden founded the Central Library, set on foot a system of free State aided libraries and reading rooms in all parts of the State, organized travelling libraries, an agency for imparting visual instruction to the illiterate masses. He also established the first library class in India"[7].

The Maharaja felt the need for trained manpower to manage the public libraries in the State. At the instance of Maharaja, Borden with the help of Clarke started the first Library School in1911, in the formal sense, to train personnel working in the public libraries[8]. The training class consisted 10 best workers of the library. The duration for the theory classes was for one year and trainees underwent practice for one more year. A short-term training programme of 5 months duration was also started by Borden for town and village librarians working in the State and outside the State. The Course contents consisted viz., Book Selection, Ordering, Accessioning, classifying, Lending, Preparing Quarterly and Annual Reports, Children's Libraries and Mobile Libraries[9].

1.4. PUNJAB SCHOOL

The second important milestone in the history of development of LIS education in the country at the university level was Punjab University, Lahore (now in Pakistan) which started a course on Library Science in 1915. The credit of starting a course on Librarianship goes to A. Dickinson, the University Librarian. The course contents among other things include: Decimal Classification, Cataloguing Rules, List of Subject Headings, Dictionary Catalogue and Open Shelves. The duration of course was for 3 months. He also wrote the first book on librarianship *"The Punjab Library Primer"* [10] which was published in 1916 by the University of the Panjab, Lahore.

The *Library Primer* consists 33 chapters with an index. These Chapters deal with: Function and spirit of the Library, the librarian and his training, the library site building and furniture, book selection and buying, checking bills, marking ownership, preparing books for use, classification, author book numbers, library hand writing, the accession and withdrawal of books. The catalogue — author, title and subject entries, library regulations, the charging system, library supplies, the care of books, reference books, periodical and periodical indexes, children, school, college and university libraries, the local history collection, the librarian's professional periodicals and books, the librarian's cultural reading, library associations, library extension, libraries of the Panjab and Indian public documents"[11].

It was stated that Labhu Ram a student of Dickinson later revised the course contents which include (a) Foreign languages, (b) Linguistic survey of India, (c) Basic Selection, (d) Law of copyright in England and India, (e) A survey from Tennyson to Bernard Shaw, (f) Sources of provincial histories of India, (g) Oriental Bibliography, (h) Milestones of English literature, (i) Library buildings, their designs and equipment, (j) Anglo-Indian literature, and (k) Open access and technical libraries. The said course continued until 1947 with certain changes to meet the requirement of changing times. The duration of the course was 6 months with graduation as minimum qualification for admission. This course gradually had shown the path towards maturation of LIS as a discipline[12].

REFERENCES

1. *The Oxford English Dictionary*, 2nd Edn. Oxford, Clarendon Press, 1989, V.5. P.74.
2. *http://en.wikipedia.org/wiki/education.#universitysystem.* Accessed on 28.08.2013.
3. Vedprakash. Universities need to become knowledge power houses (Convocation Address). *University News*, V50, N.23, June 4-10, 2012, P.19.

4. *http://www.abc.dic.com/ODLIS/odlis_a.aspec.* Accessed on 18.09.2013.

5. Krishan Kumar and Sharma, Jaideep. Library and Information Science Education in India: A Historical Perspective. *DESIDOC Journal of Library and Information Technology.* V30, N5, Sept. 2010. P.3.

6. Chakravarthy, N. C. Lest we fortget-2. Pioneers' who are no more. *ILA Bulletin.* V3, N2, April-June 1967. P.98.

7. Dutt, Newton Mohan. Baroda and its Libraries. Baroda, Central Library, 1928. Pp.2-3.

8. Nelgol, Shankar Band Kumbhar, B. D. Maharaja Shri Sayaji Rao Gaekwad III and his contribution in Library Science Education in India. In LIS Education, Research and Training: Vision 2020. Papers of 28th National Seminar 2011, IATLIS, Patiala DLISc, Panjab University, 2011. P.25.

9. Krishan Kumar and Sharma, Jaideep. *Opcit. P.4.*

10. Kurshid, Anis. Intellectual Foundation of Library Education. *Int.Lib.Sc.,* V8, 1976. P.3-21.

11. Dickinson AsaDon, The Panjab Library Primer, Lahore, University of Panjab, 1976. Pp.I-II.

12. Agarwal, S. P. *et.al.* Dictionary of LIS Education in India. New Delhi, Reliance, 1996. Pp.1-2.

2

Contribution of Library Associations

The Library Associations in the Country have played a prominent role in the growth of LIS Education in the Country during the first three decades of the 20th Century. These associations realized the need for offering professional training to the personnel working mostly in public libraries established by voluntary organizations. Mention may be made of the pioneering work done by the Andhra Desa Library Association (ADLA) (1914), Madras Library Association (MALA) (1928), Bengal Library Association (BLA) (1933) and scores of other Library Associations at the local level.

2.1. ANDHRA DESA LIBRARY ASSOCIATION (ADLA) (1914)

Andhradesa Library Association (ADLA) now (APLA) is the first professional organization for the entire Country which was established in the year 1914, at Bezawada (now Vijayawada), Andhra Pradesh. It played a prominent role for the genesis and spread of library movement in Andhradesa. Since its inception the Association recognized the importance of trained and competent professional librarians to manage the public libraries established during the thick of the library movement. Right from 1920's – 1960's the Association conducted two courses via: *1. Grandhalaya Pravesika* and *2. Grandhalaya Visarada*. The duration of the *'Pravesika'* course was thirty days. The Course content include: Library Organisation, Library Administration, Special Libraries, History of Telugu Literature and Social Sciences. The duration of 'Visarada' Course was for 3 months with full professional training[1].

The 'Pravesika' course was conducted between the years 1929 and 1962 at places such as Bezawada (1920 and 1934), Patamata (1941), Revendrapadu (1943-1945), Peda Palem (1946), Garikapuram (1948), Jaggapuram (1955), Peda Palem (1956) and Moida Vijayarampuram (962). The Visarada course was conducted just for 2 years only i.e. 1954 and 1956. The classes were held at Vijayawada (1954) and Pedapalem (1956). It also started a Certificate Course of 5 months duration and being conducted at its headquarters Vijayawada since 1966 both in Telugu and English. The Course was recognized by the Government of Andhra Pradesh[2].

Iyyanki Venkata Ramanayya, one of the pioneers of Andhra Desa Library Movement stated that under his headship the first Library School was started in 1920 for a month's duration at Ramamohan Library, Bezawada. The second School was conducted in 1934 from May 31 to June 28, at Divyajnana Samaja Mandiram, Vijayawada. The third Library School "Grandhalaya Sastra Sikshna" was organized during November 26, 1944 and December 10, 1944 at Sri Bramaramba Malleshwara Andhra Grandhalayam, Vijayawada under the auspices of Andhra Desa

Grandhalaya Sevaka Maha Sangham. Later several Library Schools were organized at several places in Andhradesa such as *Visakhapatnam (Sri Sarada Grandhalayam), Chinavindra Kolanu (West Godavari District and Machilipatnam (Krishna District),* to train the Library Workers. These library training classes organized by Andhradesa Grandhalaya Sangham and Andhradesa Grandhalaya Sevaka Mahasangham have greatly contributed to the meet the requirements of trained library workers and spread of library movement in Andhra Desa[3].

2.2. MADRAS LIBRARY ASSOCIATION (MALA) (1928)

Madras Presidency (before Independence) is one of leading provinces of India for the spread of library movement and genesis of LIS education in the Country. The Madras Library Association (MALA) established in the year 1928 sown the seeds for the genesis of LIS education especially in South India. Dr. S. R. Ranganathan in the year 1929 started 'Annual Summer School' of librarianship under the auspices of Madras Library Association. The duration of the course was for 3 months and the subjects taught were: Laws of Librarianship, Classification, Cataloguing, Issue Methods and Library Routines. After two years i.e. in 1931, the Summer School was taken over by the University of Madras. In the year 1937-38 three months course was converted into a full time diploma course of one year duration, 'supposed to be the first of its kind in India'[4]. S. R. Ranganathan taught Library Science from 1931-1946 until his retirement. Persons working in libraries were admitted to the Course.

2.3. BENGAL LIBRARY ASSOCIATION (BLA) (1925)

In Eastern India Bengal Library Association (BLA) formed in the year 1925 sowed the seeds of education for librarianship to serve the interests of working librarians. Bengal Library Association in collaboration with Hoogly District Library Association started the first library science training camp for working librarians at Bansberia, near Kolkata, in June 1934. This was a two week training programme and attended by 12 participants. The BLA started a month long summer training programme for the award of certificate on April 30, 1937 at Asutosh College. Twenty candidates were admitted for the said course of which 17 were successful. Certificates were awarded on 24th July 1937. In 1939, BLA shifted its training programme from Asutosh College to the Calcutta University Campus. Dr. Nihar Ranjan Roy, the then Librarian of Calcutta University was the Director for the Course.

In 1951 another section was opened and the students' strength was doubled. Sri B. S. Kesavan, Librarian, National Library was made the Course Director. Apart from the summer course BLA introduced a weekend course of 7 months duration in 1955. At present BLA is running these two programmes with an intake of 65 candidates for each course[5].

The system is still continuing and a certificate is awarded to successful candidates. At present, the Association manages three sections with a student strength of 180. The Association worked as a resource centre for newly formed Department of Public Libraries of the State Government as a result of enactment of Public Library Law and the expansion of Public Library System in the State[6].

2.4. OTHER LIBRARY ASSOCIATIONS

In addition to above mentioned Library Associations there are few other Associations which have contributed the growth of LIS education in the Country before and after independence. For example in 1983 Gomanthak Grandhalaya Sangh was established in Goa under the able leadership of B. D. Satorkar. It has been established on the lines of Maharashtra Rajya Grandhalaya Sangh. One of the main objectives of Gomanthak Grandhalaya Sangh was "to provide facilities for the training of qualified librarians. To fulfill this objective the Sangh since 1985 has been conducting a Certificate Course in Library Science[7].

Another Library Association which started Courses in Library Science was the Haryana Library Association which was established at Ambala in 1967. The Association conducted a certificate course in Library Science of six months duration at State Central Library from 1972-77. The said Course was recognized by the Government of Haryana for recruitment to jobs in the State[8]. The Maharashtra Rajya Grandhalaya Sangh which was established in 1962 also conducts Library Training Courses for the benefit of professionals in the State[9].

The Uttar Pradesh Library Association (UPLA) has been conducting four-month duration certificate course in Library Science since 1959. The Government of U.P. has recognized this Course since 1971 and examinations are conducted by the Registrar, Departmental Examinations, Department of Education. The Association has been conducting training courses at its 13 branches at different district headquarters. The minimum qualification required for admission to the Course was Intermediate of any recognized institution. Each year about 560 students are admitted to this Course, of which 80 seats are made available at Lucknow and 40 seats each at the remaining districts[10].

Mysore State

In the year 1920, a Course for the training of librarians was conducted at Bangalore under the Programme of Library Development due to the untiring efforts of the then Dewan of Mysore State Sri M. Vish Veswarayya[11].

REFERENCES

1. Sarada, K. *Andhra Pradesh Library Association.* Visakhapatnam, Andhra University Press, 1978. P.83.
2. Ibid, Pp.84-85.
3. Venkataramanayya, Iyyanki. *Grandhalaya Jyoti.* Vijayawada, Saraswati Samrajyam, 1967. Pp. 313-322.
4. Ramesh Babu, B. Centenary of LIS Education Research and Training in Tamil Nadu: State-of-the-Art. *In LIS Education, Research and Training: Vision 2020.* IATLIS 2011. Patiala, Panjabi University, 2011.P.443.
5. Saha, Ramakrishna. Library Movement in West Bengal. *In Library Movement in India,* Ed. by Ramakrishna Saha. Kolkata, BLA, 1998. Pp. 153-159.
6. Ray, Arun. Bengal Library Association. *In Souvenir* published on the occasion of the 34th All India Library Conference of ILA and 13th National Conference of IASLIC, 20-23 December, 1988. Ed. by Ramakrishna Saha, Calcutta, BLA, 1988. Pp.149-152.
7. Rodrigues, P.M. Library Movement in Goa. *In Souvenir.* Ibid. Pp.57-61.
8. Janakraj: Library Movement in Haryana. *In Souvenir.* Op.cit. Pp.66-70.
9. Mahajan, S. G. Library Movement in Maharashtra. *In Souvenir,* Op.cit. Pp.89-94.
10. Srivatsava, Rochana, *et al.* Library Movement in Uttar Pradesh: A State of the Art. *In Souvenir Op.cit.* Pp.129-134.
11. Kumar, P.S.G. Education for Librarianship in India.... *In Library and Information Science in India. Ed.* by P.S.G. Kumar and C. P. Varisth. P.18.

3

LIS Education in the Universities

3.1. BEFORE INDEPENDENCE

Before independence LIS education in the Country started slowly but steadily in few Universities. As stated already Panjab University at Lahore started a Certificate Course in LIS in 1915 and thus sown the seeds of genesis and development of LIS education in the Country. Asa Don Dickenson introduced this Course and thus became the first person to introduce the Course at the University level. The duration was later extended to six months[1,2].

Madras Library Association (MALA) started a three month training programme in 1929. During the year 1931, the Classes were shifted to the University of Madras. In the year 1935, due to the efforts of Dr. M. O. Thomas, the Librarian of Andhra University started a diploma Course in Library Science. Thus Andhra University became the first University in the Country to start a diploma course in Library Science. In 1937-38, S. R. Ranganathan took initiative and the Madras University converted the three months Course into a

P. G. Diploma Course of one year duration. Admission to the course was restricted to graduate librarians deputed by the concerned libraries. S. R. Ranganathan and his other colleagues in the University Library conducted the Course. Thus University of Madras became the first University in the pre-independent India to start a P.G. Course at the University level in LIS.

Banaras Hindu University (BHU) followed suit and became the second University in the Country to introduce P.G. Diploma Programme in LIS in 1941. In 1943 University of Bombay started Diploma Course in LIS and admitted graduates as well as non-graduates to the Course. It was a part-time Course for working men. The credit of introducing LIS Course goes to Dr. P. M. Joshi, the then University Librarian of University of Bombay[3]. In the year 1945 University of Calcutta introduced one year diploma course. Admission to the Course was open to graduates and the intake was limited to 15 students. This was first University to start a P.G. Course in LIS in the eastern part of the Country[4].

3.2. AFTER INDEPENDENCE

After independence in 1947, the Country witnessed steady growth in LIS Education in the Universities. Many Universities came forward and initiated action to introduce LIS courses to meet the emerging needs of trained manpower to manage public, academic and special libraries being established through the length and breadth of Country. These Universities started offering P. G. Diploma in LIS and later BLIS / MLIS (One year each), MLISc (2-years integrated course) and research degrees leading to M.Phil and Ph.D. programmes. There were few instances where D.Lit degrees were awarded in LIS by the Universities based on original contribution.

North India

North India constitute the States of Uttar Pradesh, Uttaranchal, Jammu and Kashmir, Panjab, Haryana, Delhi and the Union territory of Chandigarh. There are several Universities in these States, both State and Central, where LIS Courses are being offered at different levels such as 1-year BLISc, 1-year MLISc, 2-year integrated MLISc and research courses such as M.Phil and Ph.D.

Uttar Pradesh is the largest State in the Indian Union. Banaras Hindu University, Varanasi is one of the oldest Universities in the Country which was founded in 1916 by Pandit Madan Mohan Malaviya. In the year 1941, the University introduced Diploma in Library Science Course. BLISc was introduced in 1961. In the year 1965 the University started M.Lib.Sc., the second Course for the entire Country after University of Delhi. It introduced 2-year integrated MLISc Course and started Ph.D. programme in the year 1980. Next to follow was Aligarh Muslim University, Aligarh which started 1-year BLIS in the year 1958 and MLISc in the year 1970. The University also introduced research courses leading to the award of M.Phil and Ph.D. degrees in the year 1990. In the year 2005 the University introduced 2 year integrated MLISc Course in place of 1 year BLISc and 1 year MLISc.

Lucknow University was established in the year 1920 and the University introduced LIS Courses in the year 1972. Presently the University offers 1 year BLISc, 1-year MLISc and Ph.D. programme in LIS. Dr. B. R. Ambedkar University, Agra, earlier known as Agra University started LIS Courses in the year 1984. Presently this University offers 1-year BLISc, 1-year MLISc and Ph.D. programmes in LIS. Bundelkhand University, Jhansi came into being in the year 1975.

The University introduced 1-year BLIS, 1-year MLISc and M.Phil and Ph.D. Courses in the year 1984. Babasaheb Bhimrao Ambedkar University, Lucknow, a Central University, established the Department of Library &Information Science in the year 1997 and it is offering 2-year MLISc Course and Ph.D. programme.

The University of Kashmir, Srinagar was established in the year 1969 and the University is offering 2-year MLISc, M.Phil and Ph.D. programmes in LIS. The University of Jammu came into being in the year 1969. During the academic year 1983-84, the University introduced 1-year BLISc Programme and from the academic year MLISc and Ph.D. programmes were introduced.

Punjab University was located at Chandigarh, a centrally administered City in1956. The University started BLISc Course from the academic year 1968-69, BLISc from 1988-89, MLISc from 1970-71 and Ph.D. from 1972-73. The University introduced 2-year MLISc Course from the Academic year 2003-04.

University of Delhi was established in the year 1922, now a Central University. The Department of Library Science was established in the year 1946 due to initiative taken by Dr. S. R. Ranganathan. Post-graduate Diploma Course in LIS was started in the year 1947. It started MLISc Course in the year 1948 and Ph.D. Programme, for the first time in the Country, in the year 1952. Presently this University offers 1-year BLISc, 1-year MLISc, M.Phil in the year 1978.

Jamia Millia Islamia Delhi, was declared as a Central University by an Act of Parliament in the year 1988. The University introduced BLISc Course in the year 1985.

In the State of Panjab only two Universities were

offering courses in LIS. Panjabi University, Patiala was established in 1962. The University established the Department of Library and Information Science in the year 1969. The University started 1-year BLISc Course in 1986 and MLISc in 1989 and also offers Ph.D. in LIS. Guru Nanak Dev University, Amritsar was established in the year 1969. The Department of Library & Information Science was established in the year 1970. It started 1-year BLISc in the year 1969 and 1-year MLIS in the year 1984. The University also offers M.Phil and Ph.D. Programmes in LIS.

In Haryana only two Universities viz. 1. Kurukshetra University and 2. Maharishi Dayanand University were offering courses in LIS. Kurukshetra University, Kurukshetra was established in the year 1956 and Department of Library and Information Science was established in the year 1969. Presently the University offers courses such as 1-year BLISc, 1-year MLISc, M.Phil and Ph.D. on a regular basis. Maharishi Dayanand University, Rohtak was established in the year 1976. Presently this University offers 1-year BLISc, 1-year MLISc Courses through the Directorate of Distance Education (DDE)[5].

The new State of Uttarakhand came into being on 7th November 2000. At present there are five Universities in the State viz. 1. HNB Garhwal University, Srinagar (Central University), 2. Himagirijee University (Private University), 3. Uttarakhand Sanskrit University, Haridwar (State University), 4. Uttarakhand Technical University, Dehradun (State University) and 5. Kumaun University, Nainital (State University) were offering Courses in LIS leading to the award of BLISc, MLISc Degrees. Earlier Ph.D. Course in LIS was offered by HNB Garhwal University, Srinagar. But it appears that presently the said course is not offered. It appears that Uttarakhand Technical University, Dehradun is likely to introduce Ph.D. programme in LIS[6].

Especially in Haryana, Polytechnic Colleges were offering 3-year Diploma Course in LIS. The Goernment Polytechnic for Women at Ambala City, Mahila Polytechnic at Khanpur (Sonpat) and Vaish Technical Institute at Rohtak were offering Diploma Courses in LIS. It has been said that presently the said course is offered at several polytechnic colleges in the State. The minimum qualification for admission is matriculation[7].

Besides LIS Courses in the traditional Universities, the National Institute of Science Communication and Information Resources (NISCAIR), a constituent organ of CSIR was formed when INSDOC and National Institute of Science Communication (NISCOM) was merged on September 30, 2002. The Education and Training Division of NISCAIR is offering a Course in LIS called Associateship in Information Science (AIS), which they claim to be equivalent of MLISc programme offered by the Universities in the Country.

South India

As is well known that South India consists of four major States of Indian Union viz. Andhra Pradesh, Tamil Nadu, Karnataka, Kerala and Union territory of Pandicherry. These States have contributed significantly for the growth and spread of LIS education in the Country. The Universities in these States have established Departments of LIS and offering BLISc, MLISc, MLISc (2-year Integrated programme) and research courses leading to the award of M.Phil and Ph.D. programmes.

In Andhra Pradesh mention may be made of Andhra University which started Diploma Programme in 1935 and after independence, the said course was upgraded as P.G. Diploma in LIS in 1961. Osmania University is the first University in the State to offer P.G. Diploma in LIS in 1959. Sri Venkateshwara University, Tirupati followed suit and started BLISc Course in 1974. Sri Krishna Devaraya University, Anantapur started BLISc Course in 1982. Nagarjuna University, Guntur and Kakatiya University, Warangal started courses in LIS in distance mode in the year 2005 and 2004 respectively. Of late, in the year 2009 Dravidian University, Kuppam announced starting of 2-year integrated MLISc and M.Phil and Ph.D. programmes in 2009 in the regular and distance mode[8]. But the programmes have not yet been started (until 2011).

In Tamil Nadu a number of Universities have started courses in LIS such as CLIS, BLIS, MLIS, M.Phil and Ph.D. both in traditional and distance mode. As stated already University of Madras, Chennai started a PG Diploma in LIS during the year 1937-38 under the dynamic leadership of Dr. S. R. Ranganathan. In 1960 the said University started full-time PG Degree called BLISc of one year duration. Later this University in due course of time introduced MLIS and Ph.D. in LIS. For the first time this University started M.Sc Information Science under the Faculty of Science.

Madurai Kamaraj University, Madurai, started BLISc Course in 1975 and later started MLIS, M.Phil and Ph.D. programmes. Annamalai University, Annamalai Nagar, Chidambaram, introduced LIS Courses in the year 1979. Presently MLISc (2-years), M.Phil and Ph.D. programmes in LIS are offered by this University.

Alagappa University, Karaikudi introduced LIS Courses in the year 1993. Presently this University is offering BLISc, MLIS, M.Phil and Ph.D. programmes in LIS. AVM Pushpam College introduced MLISc, M.Phil and Ph.D. Courses in the year 2003. Bharatidasan University, Tiruchirapalli started LIS Courses in the year 2007 and presently this University is offering MLIS, M.Phil and Ph.D. programmes. In the year 2008 Bharathiar University, Coimbatore started MLIS, M.Phil and Ph.D. programmes in LIS. The Bishop Hebbar College, Tiruchirapally started MLIS Course in the year 1983[9].

The above mentioned Universities were also offering the Courses in LIS in the distance mode. In addition to these Universities, there were other Universities in Tamil Nadu such as: Mother Terasa University (1984), Kodaikannal Manonmaniam Sundarnar University (1990) Tirunelveli, Periyar University (2009) Salem, St. Peters University (2009) Chennai, Karunaya University (2008) Coimbatore, Vinayaka Mission (2006) Salem were offering Courses in Library Science in the distance mode. Anna University, Chennai, a technological university, which has no Department of Library & Information Science, has at its campuses in Madurai, Coimbatore, Tiruchirapalli, have been offering Ph.D. programmes in LIS in the distance education mode. Sri Chandrasekharendra Saraswati Vishwa Maha Vidyalaya University, Kanchipuram also offering Ph.D. programmes in LIS[10].

In Karnataka there are seven Universities which were offering courses in LIS. Mysore University, Mytsore was the first University in the State to start courses in LIS in the year 1965. Presently it is offering MLISc (2-years) and Ph.D. programme on regular basis. Next to follow suit was Karnatak University, Dharwad which started the Course in LIS in the year 1962.

Presently the University is offering 2 year MLIS Course and M.Phil and Ph.D. programmes on regular basis. Next to follow is Bangalore University, Bangalore which started Course in LIS in the year 1974. Presently the said University is offering MLISc (2-years) and Ph.D. programme in LIS. Gulbarga Universityl, Gulbarga started LIS Courses in the year 1980. Presently this University is offering 2-year MLISc programme along with M.Phil and Ph.D. programmes on regular basis, Mangalore University, Mangalore started LIS Courses in the year 1982. Presently this University is offering 2-years MLISc Course and Ph.D. programme on regular basis. Kuvempu University started LIS Course in the year 1993. Presently this University is offering BLISc (1-year), MLISc (2-years) and M.Phil and Ph.D. programmes. Tumukur University, Tumukur started courses in LIS in the year 2005. Presently this University is offering MLISc (2-years) and Ph.D programme on regular basis. Karnataka State Women's University started LIS courses in the year 2007. Presently this University is offering MLISc (2-years) and Ph.D. programme on regular basis.

In Kerala, the smaller State in South India, three Universities were offering courses in LIS. University of Kerala, Trivandrum was the first University in the State which started courses in LIS in the year 1962. Presently this University offers MLIS (2-years) and research courses like M.Phil and Ph.D. programmes on regular basis. University of Calicut, Calicut, was the second University in the State to start courses in LIS in the year 1978. Presently this University offers 2-years MLIS Programme besides M.Phil and Ph.D. programmes in LIS. Kannuru University is the third University in the State which started courses in LIS in the year 2009. This University is offering MLISc (2-years) and Ph.D.

programme on regular basis. In the Union territory of Pondicherry, Pondicherry University, a Central University, started offering 2-years MLISc programme from the year 2007. Besides this, University is also offering PGD Lan[11].

East and Northeast India

The East and Northeast India consists of ten States viz: West Bangal, Odisha, Arunachal Pradesh, Assam, Manipur, Meghalaya, Mizoram, Nagaland, Thripura and Sikkim. Among these ten States, LIS Courses are not offered in Arunachal Pradesh and Nagaland. In the rest of the eight States of E-NE, the Universities in the respective States have been offering courses in LIS at different levels with varied degree of difference and standard.

In the West Bengal, the leading State in Eastern and Northeastern India, LIS course was started as far back as 1945 at Calcutta University one of the oldest Universities in the Country. As stated already Diploma course in LIS was started at Calcutta University in the year 1945 i.e. before independence of the Country. Presently this University is offering 1-year BLISc, 2-years MLISc and 2-years M.Phil programme. The next to follow was Jadavpur University, Kolkata which introduced courses in LIS in the year 1964. Presently this University is offering 1-year BLISc, 1-year MLISc, 2-years M.Phil and 2-years part-time MLISc in the distance mode. The University of Burdwan. Burdwan, introduced courses in LIS in the year 1965. Presently the University offers courses in LIS consisting 1-year BLISc, 1-year MLISc, and M.Phil. Vidyasagar University, Midnapur introduced courses in LIS in the year 1985. Presently this University is offering 1-year BLISc, 1-year MLISc and 2-years M.Phil programmes.

Rabindra Bharati University, Kolkata introduced LIS courses in the year 1985. Presently this University is offering 1-year BLISc and 1-year MLISc progrmmes. North Bengal University started courses in LIS in the year 1990. Presently this University is offering 1-year BLISc,and 1-year MLISc courses. Kalyani University started LIS courses in the year 1990 and currently offering 1-year BLISc, 1-year MLISc and 1-year M.Phil programmes in distance mode.

In Odisha, Sambalpur University, Burla was the first University in the State to start courses in LIS in the year 1976. Presently this University is offering 2-years MLISc and 1-year M.Phil and Ph.D. on regular basis and PGD LAN in the Distance mode. Next to follow was Utkal University at Bhubaneshwar, the State Capital. This University started courses in the year 1981 and presently offering 2-years MLISc Programme and Ph.D. Course. Sanjay Memorial Institute of Technology (SMIT), Ankuspur, near Berhampur, introduced 1-year BLISc and 1-year MLISc course in the year 1983. This Institute is affiliated to Berhampur University. North Odisha University started Courses in LIS in the year 2003. Presently this University is offering 2-years MliSc on regular basis and BLISc in the distance mode.

In Assam, Gauhati University, Guwahati was the first University to introduce courses in LIS in the year 1966. This University is offering 2-years MLISc courses. Next to follow was Dibrugarh University, Dibrugarh which started courses in LIS in the year 2005 and offering 1-year BLISc and 1-year MLISc courses. In the year 2009, Assam University, Silchar, started courses in LIS and offering 2-years MLISc course. In Meghalaya, Northeastern Hill University (NEHU), Shillong started programme in the year 1985 and currently offering 2-

years MLISc course and also Ph.D. programme. Manipur University, Imphal introduced courses in LIS in the year 1986 and currently offering 2-years MLISc programme. Mizoram University, Aijwal, started LIS course in the year 2002 and currently offering 2-years MLISc course. Tripura University, Agartal was established in the year 1987. BLISc course was started during the academic year 2010-11 at Ramthakur College affiliated to Tripura University. In Sikkim, Sikkim University a Central University was established in the year 2007. In D. S. College, Gangtok one of its affiliated colleges 1-year BLISc course was introduced in the year 2004[12].

Western India

Western India consists of States of Maharasthra, Gujarat and Rajasthan. In Maharashtra, Bombay University (now University of Mumbai) is one of the oldest Universities in the country and was established during the British rule in the year 1857. This University started a course in LIS in the year 1944 and presently offers 1-year BLISc, 1-year MLISc and Ph.D. programme. Next to follow was RTM Nagpur University (1923), Nagpur which started a course in LIS in the year 1956. This is the oldest University in the Vidarbha region of Maharasthra. Presently this University offers 2-years MLISc and research courses such as M.Phil and Ph.D. There are fourteen colleges affiliated to Nagpur University, offering BLIS, MLISc Courses. University of Pune (1948), Pune which was established after independence, presently offers 2-years MLISc, M.Phil and Ph.D. programmes. SNDT Women's University (1916), Mumbai one of the oldest Women's Universities in the country started LIS courses in the year 1961. Presently this Univerity is offering courses such as 1-year BLISc, 1-year MLISc and Ph.D.

programme in LIS. Shivaji University (1962), Kolhapur started courses in LIS in the year 1965. Presently this University offers courses such as: 1-year BLISc, 1-year MLISc and Ph.D. programme in LIS. Dr. Babasaheb Ambedkar Marathwada University (1958), Aurangabad, started a course in LiS in the year 1968. Presently this University offers 2-years MLISc and M.Phil and Ph.D. programmes in LIS.

Sant Gadge Baba Amravati University (1983), Amravati started a course in LIS in the year 1990. Presently this University offers 1-year BLISc, 1-year MLIS and Ph.D. programme. Swami Ramanandthirth Maratwada University (1994), Nanded is one of young Universities in Maratwada region of the State. This University started LIS course in the year 1999 and presently offering 2-years MLISc and Ph.D. programmes in LIS. North Maharasthra University (1989), Jalgaon started LIS course in the year 2000. Presently this University offers only 2-years MLISc Programme. Besides these nine Universities, Tilak Maharasthra Vidyapeeth, Pune, Bharati Vidya Pith, Deemed University, Pune and Yashwantrao Chavan Maharasthra Open University, Nashik offer courses in LIS[13].

In Gujarat State there are eight Universities which offer courses in LIS. These are: 1. M.S. University, Baroda, 2. Gujarat University, Ahmedabad, 3. Saurastra University, Rajkot, 4. Sardar Patel University, Vallabh Vidyanagar, 5. Gujarat Vidyapeeth, Ahmedabad, 6. Bhavnagar University, Bhavnagar, 7. Veer Narmad South Gujarat University, Surat and 8. Hemchandracharya North Gujarat University, Patan. The credit of first starting LIS Course goes to M. S. University, Baroda, although Gujarat Vidyapeet is the oldest University in the State.

Almost all Universities in the State offer 1-year BLISc, 1-year MLISc or 2-years MLISc and research courses like M.and Ph.D. Sardar Patel University and Veer Narmad South Gujarat University offer 2-year part-time MLISc course. On the other hand Gujarat University and Gujarat Vidyapeeth offer 2-years integrated MLISc course. Sardar Patel University, Gujarat Vidyapeeth and Hemachandra Charya North Gujarat University offer M.Phil programme. Most of these Universities offer Ph.D. degree in LIS[14].

In Rajasthan, the University of Rajasthan, Jaipur established the Department of Library and Information Science in the year 1960 and introduced BLISc course in 1961, and MLISc and Ph.D. courses in the year 1974. The second University in the State to introduce courses in LIS was the University of Udaipur (now Mohanlal Sukhadia University) which started BLISc course during the academic year 1975-76 and introduced MLISc course in the year 1995-96[15]. In addition to these two Universities Jai Narayan Vyas University, Jodhpur offers BLISc course on regular basis. Some of the Colleges such as Arya Vidyapeeth Kanya Maha Vidyalaya, Bhusawer, Lal Bahadur Sastri College, Jaipur and Mahatma Jyoti Pule Girls College, Jaipur offers BLISc course on regular basis. Kota Open University, Kota offers Ph.D. programme in LIS[16].

Central India

The Central India constitutes two States viz: Madhya Pradesh and Chhattisgarh. The new State of Chhatisgarh was carved out from Madhya Pradesh. In Madhya Pradesh there are eight Universities, including, an Open University offering courses in LIS. Among these Universities, Doctor Harising Gaur Vishwavidyalaya, Sagar is the oldest University established in the year 1946. This was made Central University in the year 2009. It introduced LIS courses in the year 1970 and offering BLISc, MLISc and Ph.D. programmes. The second University to be established was Rani Durgavati Vishwa Vidyalaya, which was established in the year 1959 at Jabalpur. This University initially introduced courses in LIS at K. P. Guru Bhasha Bharati in the 1970s. From 2002 the University introduced 2-years MLISc programme. Devi Ahilya Vishwa Vidyalaya, Indore was established in the 1964. During the Academic year 1993-94 BLISc course was introduced as part-time course. From the year 2006, the University started 1-year BLISc and 1-year MLISc as regular courses. M.Phil course was introduced from the academic year 2009-10. Jiwaji University, Gwalior was established in the year 1964. In the year 1984, the University introduced 1-year BLISc, 1-year MLIS courses and also Ph.D. programme. Awadesh Pratap Singh University, Rewa, was established in the year 1968. Presently it offers 1-year BLISc and 1-year MLISc courses in LIS. Makhanlal Chaturvedi Rashtriya Patrakarita Vishwavidyalaya was sestablished in the year 1990 at Bhopal, the capital city of Madhya Pradesh. At its NOIDA Campus the University offers 1-year BLISc course. It also offers Ph.D. in LIS. Mahatma Gandhi Chitrakoot Gramodaya Vishwa Vidyalaya was established in the year 1991. It offers courses in LIS as part of its academic programmes in the distance mode. Madhya Pradesh Bhoj Open University was established in the year 1991. The University introduced 1-year BLISc, 1-year MLISc courses through the distance mode. Vikram University, Ujjain also offers BLISc, MLISc asnd Ph.D. courses on regular basis.

In addition to these institutions of higher learning,

Barkatullah Viswavidyalaya, Bhopal, offers BLISc / MLISc courses in distance mode. Govt. Girls College, Gwalior, Government MLB Arts & Commerce College, Gwalior offers BLISc and MLISc courses on regular basis. In addition Kamta Prasad & Guru Bhasha Bharati, Jabalpur, Lal Bhadur Sastri College, Gwalior and Rajeev Gandhi College, Bhopal offer BLISc course on regular basis. The Army Education Core (AEC) Training College & Centre, Pachmarhi also offers BLISc course. These Colleges are affiliated to the respective Universities[17].

In Chattisgarh only two Universities viz: Guru Ghasidas Vishwa Vidyalaya, Bilaspur and Pandit Ravi Shankar Shukla University, Raipur were offering PG level Courses in LIS.[18] Guru Ghasidas Vishwa Vidyalaya was established in 1983 and became a Central University by an Act of Parliament in 2009. Pandit Ravishankar Shukla University, the oldest University in the State was established in the year 1964. The Dept. of LIS of Guru Ghasidas Vishwa Vidyalaya was established in the year 1985 and that of Pandit Ravishankar Shukla University was established in the year 1971. The former offers only BLISc and the later MLISc courses[19].

Bihar and Jharkhand

In Bihar Patna University, Patna, offers only BLISc course on regular and in distance mode. On the other hand Tilak Manjhi Bhagalpur University, Bhagalpur offers BLISc / MLISc courses on regular basis. Lalit Narayan Mithila University, Dharbanga offers BLISc on regular basis. National Open University, Patna, offers only BLISc on distance mode. In Jharkhand Birla Institute of Technology (popularly klnown as BITS), Mesra, Ranchi, offers integrated 2-years MLISc in Information Science[20].

3.3. OTHER INSTITUTIONS

In addition to Courses offered at semi-professional level by the Library Associations and professional level by the LIS Departments / Schools of the Universities in the Country, there are few other institutions, other than Universities, which were offering courses in LIS by awarding degrees such as Associateship / Masters Degree.

In this regard mention may be made of INSDOC (now merged with NISCOM), New Delhi and DRTC, Bangalore which have been offering Courses in LIS leading to the award of Associateship in Documentation / Information Science (ADIS) or Master of Science in Library and Information Science (MS-LIS). But these two institutions were not offering research courses leading to the award of M.Phil / Ph.D. degrees in LIS. The following paras briefly deal with NISCAIR and DRTC.

Indian National Scientific Documentation Centre (INSDOC), New Delhi

INSDOC, Indian National Scientific Documentation Centre was established in the year 1952, as constituent unit of the Council of Scientific and Industrial Research (CSIR) of India to provide efficient and comprehensive information services, specializes in information management, develops human resources in information and documentation science and carries out research in information science and technology.

INSDOC has been offering an advanced training course in Documentation and Reprography since August 1964. The Course was renamed as Associateship in Information Science in 1977, keeping in mind the changing context of information requirements.

The Education and Training Division of INSDOC organizes and over sees all the activities relating to the conduct of the Associateship and short term courses. INSDOC claimed that the programme is of two year duration, out of which first one year is devoted to teaching of the eight papers as prescribed in the syllabus. The second year is devoted to Papers-9 and 10 which deal with project works and dissertation respectively. The Prospectus and Syllabus (1990) claims that Associateship in Information Science as "A Post-Graduate level Course". There was debate as to whether the INSOC's course can be treated on par with the MLISc Course offered by the Universities in India. Majority of the Indian Universities have not recognized the Course on par with their MLISc programmes for academic purposes i.e. for pursuing M.Phill and Ph.D. Programmes

Merger of INSDOC with NISCOM

As per the recommendations of the CSIR Review Committee headed by Prof. Abid Hussain, INSDOC and NISCOM (National Institute of Science Communication) were merged together to form a single entity called NISCAIR (National Institute of Science Communication and Information Resources) with effect from 30th September 2002. One of the major functions of NISCAIR was to develop human resources in the field of Science Communication, Library and Information Science, Documentation and S & T Information Management Systems and Services.

After the merger of INSDOC with NISCAIR, the course "Associateship in Information Science" earlier conducted by INSDOC was discontinued. But the

Journal *Annals of Library and Information Studies* is being continued as quarterly publication. Presently this Journal publishes "Original contnributions, survey reports, reviews, short communications and letters" pertaining to LIS and related aspects. This journal on its own way contributed to the growth and development of LIS education in the Country[21].

Documentation Research and Training Centre (DRTC), Bangalore

The Documentation Research and Training Centre (DRTC) was established in the year 1962 as a division of the Indian Statistical Institute (ISI). The objectives of DRTC are as follows:

1. To perform and promote research in the Documentation and Library Science in general.
2. To train senior documentalists needed for service in the Country and in other Developing Countries, and
3. To provide Consultant Service in Documentation.

Initially DRTC offered a 'two year programme' called Associateship in Documentation and Information Science (ADIS). Since 2008-2010 ADIS has been changed to Master of Science in Library and Information Science (MS-LIS). This Course offers instruction in Theory and Practice of Documentation and Information Science. It also consists of Project Works, Colloquia, Seminars, Lectures and Practicals.

In addition, DRTC organizes an All-India Seminar in mid-December each year to keep up continuing research and to exchange ideas with practicing documentalists, senior professors and research workers on the subject of current interest. Right from 1963 DRTC has been conducting these seminars. Since

1969 it is conducting refresher seminar every year in the month of May.

DRTC has been collaborating with the Sarada Ranganathan Endowment for Library Science in bringing out the quarterly journal *Library Science with a slant to Documentation* (1964-87). In due course the title of the journal change twice as: *Library Science with a slant to Documentation and Information Studies* (1988-1999) and presently as: *SRELS Journal of Information Management bimonthly*[22].

This journal has been publishing, since its inception, scholarly articles on various facets of LIS education in the country and opened up its pages to the senior as well as junior LIS teachers and professionals to air their views on various aspects of LIS education in the Country.

3.4. PROLIFERATION OF LIS SCHOOLS

After independence LIS Education in India slowly gained momentum and a large number of Universities established Departments of LIS without proper infrastructure facilities, required staff and library facilities. This uncontrolled growth of LIS Schools in the Universities and other institutions effected the quality of LIS Education. Prof. Kaula observed that "more and more institutions and libraries are opening library science courses without having even the minimum facilities for teaching. Even with poor libraries and funds, they have started MLISc programmes. In some Universities there are no full-time teachers to teach BLISc Courses and yet some of them started MLISc programme. Open Universities have also started B.Lib.Sc. programme. The uncontrolled growth has brought down the standard of the Courses. Library Associations have also been having a large intake of students without assessing the employment opportunities of the products"[23]. Commenting on the situation obtained in LIS Schools in India during 1980s and criticism emanating from various quarters Prof. K. A. Isaac observed that "the criticism is based on several grounds like inadequate course content, unsatisfactory teaching arrangements and learning facilities, low caliber of students entering the courses and lack of motivation in them and so on"[24].

The same situation more or less was obtaining in some of LIS Schools in India even in first decade of the present century. Courses are being started or new LIS Schools being opened without taking into consideration the infrastructure needed, qualified required staff, motivated students and lastly but not the least the updated syllabus to meet the present day requirements of various types of libraries and information centres.

As per the Table below the Country witnessed steady growth of LIS Schools in India totaling 71 up to 1980s. 1960s and 1980s witnessed establishment of more number of LIS Departments than 1950s and 1970s. 1990s also witnessed the establishment of few LIS Departments in the Indian Universities. 1990s also witnessed the proliferation Correspondence and Distance Education Institutions established by traditional universities and emergence open and distance learning universities which have started courses in LIS leading to the award of BLISc, MLISc, M.Phil and Ph.D. degrees on par with the traditional Universities. The emergence of LIS education through distance mode in India is presented in a separate Chapter.

The following Table throws some light on the number of LIS Schools in India before and after independence up to 1980s.

Table

Before 1950	1950s	1960s	1970s	1980s
1. Madras	1. Aligarh	1. SNDT	1. Saurashtra	1. Mangalore
2. Andhra	2. Nagpur	2. Rajasthan	2. Bhagalpur	2. NEHU
3. Banaras	3. Baroda	3. Kerala	3. Kashmir	3. Bharatidasan
4. Bombay	4. Vikram	4. Army Edn. Corps	4. G.N.Dev	4. Utkal
5. Calcutta	5. Punjab	5. Karnatak	5. Ravi Shnakar	5. SK University
6. Delhi	6. Poona	6. IT College	6. Mithila	6. Jamia Milia
	7. Osmania	7. MLB College	7. Lucknow	7. Ravindra Bharati
		8. Mysore	8. S.V.University	8. SB Womens College
		9. Gujarat	9. Madurai	9. Berhampur
		10. Jadavpur	10. Bangalore	10. Sardar Patel
		11. Shivaji	11. Sambalpur	11. Tilak Vidyapeeth
		12. Burdwan	12. Gulbarga	12. South Gujarat
		13. Maratwada	13. Agra	13. Kasi Vidyapeeth
		14. Varanasiya	14. Calicut	14. AP Open Uni.
		15. Punjabi	15. Jammui	15. Bundelkhand
		16. A.P.Singh		16. Bhavnagar
		17. Guwahati		17. Gujarat Vidyapeeth
		18. Jabalpur		18. Vidyasagar
		19. Udaipur		19. Amravati
		20. Kurukshetra		20. Bidya Bharati
		21. Patna		21. Manipur
		22. Sagar		22. Guru Ghasi Das

Source: PSG Kumar: Education for Librarianship in India. *In Library and Information Science in India.* Ed. by P.S.G. Kumar and C.P. Vashishth.

REFERENCES

1. Ganaie, Shabir Ahmed. LIS Education in India: Genesis and Development. *In LIS Education Research and Training: Vision 2020.* IATLIS 2011. Patiala, IATLIS, DLISc, Panjab University, 2011. Pp.42-56.
2. Krishan Kumar and Sharma, Jaideep. LIS Education in India: A Historical Perspective. *DJLIT* V30, N5, Sept.2010. Pp.3-8.

3. Ibid.
4. Panigrahi, P. LIS Education in East and North East India: Retrospect and Prospect. *DJLIT.* V30, N5, Sept. 2010. Pp.32-47.
5. Walia, Paramjeet Kaur. LIS Education in North India. *DJLIT* V30, N5, Sept. 2010. Pp.19-31.
6. Dhirman, Anilkumar. LIS Education in Uttarkhand: An Apprisal. *In LIS Education, Research and Training: Vision 2020.* IATLIS 2011. Patiala, Panjabi University, 2011. Pp.499-509.
7. Premsingh. Libraries and Library Education in Haryana on the March. *ILA Bulletin* V37, N2, June 2001. Pp.59-64.
8. Varalakshmi, R.S.R. LIS Education in South India: Perspectives and Challenges. *DJLIT* V30, N5, Sept. 2010. Pp.19-31.
9. Ramesh Babu, B. Centenary of LIS Education, Research and Training in Tamil Nadu... *In LIS Education, Research and Training: Vision 2020.* IATLIS 2011. Patiala, DLISc, Panjab University, 2011. Pp.442-454.
10. Ibid.
11. Varalakshmi, R.S.R. LIS Education in South India. *Op.cit.* Pp.19-31.
12. Sinha, Manojkumr. LIS Education and Research Scenario in North East Region of India: An overview. *In LIS Education, Research and Training: Vision 2020.* IATLIS 2011. Patiala, DLISc, Panjabi University 2011. Pp.510-530.
13. Gokhale, Pratibha. LIS Education in Maharashtra: A Perspective. *DJLIT* V30, N5, Sept.2010. Pp.48-53.
14. Pradhan, Sangha Mitra. LIS Education in Gujarat: Perspective and Challenges. *In LIS Education, Research and Training: Vision 2020.* IATLIS 2011. Patiala, DLISc, Panjabi University 2011. Pp.488-498.
15. Agarwal, V.K. Development of Library Education in Rajasthan. *In Fifty years of LIS Education in India.* Ed. by A. A. N. Raju *et.al.* Hyderabad, IATLIS, 1997. Pp.49-53.
16. Ratwani, M. R. *etal*; A Regional Study of LIS Education in India: Some Observations. *ILA Bulletin,* V38, N4, Octo-Dec., 2002. Pp.108-117.
17. Ibid.
18. Kaur, Prabhajeet and Kaur Walia, Paranjeet. LIS Education

in Chattigarh and Madhya Pradesh. *DJLIT*, V30, N5, Sept.2010. Pp.91-96.

19. Ibid.
20. Ratwani, M.R. *etal.* A Regional Study of LIS Education. *Opcit.*
21. *http://,niscain.in/home.asp.* Accessed on 20.08.2013.
22. Neelameghan, A. Documentation Research and Training Centre, Bangalore, *Encyclopedia of Library and Information Science.* V7. New York, Marcel Dekker, 1972. Pp.269-290.
23. Kaula, P.N. Hundred years of LIS Education: Evaluation and Trend. *In Library and Information Science in India. Ed.* by P. S. G. Kumar and C. P. Vashisth. New Delhi, Sterling Publications, 1992. P.10.
24. Isaack, K. A. LIS Education in India: Sinning or Sinned against. *In Librarianship and Library Science Education. Ed.* by Sewa Singh, New Delhi, Ess Ess Publications, 1988. P.80.

4

LIS Education Through Distance Mode

It is rather difficult to arrive at an accepted definition for distance education. The term is often confused with correspondence education; distance education and open education. Several attempts have been made by the experts to define the term succinctly. O. Peters defined distance education as "method of imparting knowledge, skills and attitudes which is rationalized by the application of division of labour and organizational principles as well as extensive use of technical media specially for the purpose of reproducing high quality teaching material which makes it possible to instruct great number of students at the same time wherever they live. It is an industrialized form of teaching and learning"[1].

4.1. GROWTH OF DISTANCE EDUCATION IN INDIA

Distance Education (DE) in India originated during the later part of 20th Century. During the seventies DE was attached to the conventional university education system. Some of the Universities in India established correspondence Institutes to impart education in various disciplines. In the history of DE in India, for the first time, the Government of Andhra Pradesh took a historic decision and established Andhra Pradesh Open University (now Dr. B. R. Ambedkar Open University) in the year 1982 to provide DE to the under privileged in the State. An autonomous institution at the level of a University was established to develop and expand DE in State of Andhra Pradesh. Late Prof. G. Ram Reddy was primarily instrumental and played a key role in the establishment of this University and became its first Vice-Chancellor. This development prompted other States in the Country and especially the Government of India to establish an Open University at the National level. The then Pime Minister of India Sri Rajiv Gandhi played a crucial role and lent full support for the establishment of the Indira Gandhi National Open University (IGNOU) in September 1985. Consequently several States in the Country such as Mahjarashtra, Kerala, Bihar, Madhya Pradesh, Karnataka, Tami Nadu, Rajasthan to mention few, have started establishing Open Universities to provide higher education at the doorsteps of the distance learners.

4.2. NEED FOR LIS EDUCATION THROUGH DISTANCE MODE

The following reasons were identified for the need for DE in LIS. These were:

1. To increase the required manpower in LIS to manage various types of libraries and information centres in the Country.
2. To upgrade existing knowledge and professional skills among the professionals working in different capacities in different library and information centres.

3. To remove geographical and time constraints.
4. To provide flexibility in learning process according the needs of distance learners.
5. Reduce or minimize the social, economic and cultural constraints faced by the distance learners.
6. To provide cost-effective means of enhancing professional skills and to obtain professional qualifications at different levels.
7. To provide an opportunity to climb the professional ladder and reach the higher positions in the career of distance learners[2].

In addition, Open and Distance Learning Institutions provide flexibility in combination of Courses, age of entry, pace of learning and method of evaluation[3]. It has been estimated that during the year 2009-10, as per the Distance Education Council (DEC) records, there were 532 conventional Universities in the Country and out of them 183 had correspondence course institutes / directorates of distance education. Further there were 14 Open Universities and 53 other Open Distance Learning (ODL) Institutes during the same period in the Country. The total number of ODL Institutions existed during 2009-10 had been 250[4].

4.3. OPEN AND DISTANCE LEARNING UNIVERSITIES / INSTITUTIONS OFFERING LIS COURSES

Introduction of LIS Courses by Open and Distance Learning Universities / Institutions added another dimension to the LIS Courses in India and provided opportunities for more students to pursue LIS Courses at different levels so as to upgrade their professional qualifications for better employment opportunities. This is a positive development for the spread of LIS education in the Country. But there is another view in some quarters that open and distance learning may affect the quality of LIS education and thereby producing below standard or substandard products. But open and distance education has come to stay and slowly gaining strength and expanding rapidly to offer higher education to the needy. LIS is no exception in this regard. Out of fourteen Open Universities functioning in the Country, the following nine Universities were offering LIS Course at different levels[5].

List of Open Universities offering LIS Courses

Sl. No.	Name of the Open University	Courses offered
1	Dr. B. R. Ambedkar Open University, Hyderabad	BLISc /MLISc / M.Phil / Ph.D.
2	Indira Gandhi National Open University, New Delhi	BLISc / MLISc / Ph.D.
3	Yeshwant Rao Chavan Maharasthra Open University, Nasik	BLISc/ MLISc / Ph.D.
4	Vardhman Mahaveer Open University, Kota, (Rajasthan)	BLISc /MLISc/ M.Phil / Ph.D.
5	Nalanda Open University, Patna	DLISc / BLISc
6	Karnatak Open University, Mysore	BLISc
7	U.P. Rajashree Tandon Open University, Allahabad	BLISc / MLISc
8	M.P. Bhoj University, Bhopal	BLISc /MLISc / Ph.D.
9	Dr. Baba Saheb Ambedkar Open University, Ahmedabad	BLISc

As stated earlier Dr. B. R. Ambedkar Open University, Hyderabad was the first University in the Country to start BLISc Course in the distance mode during the academic year 1984-85. It has also introduced MLISc Course during the academic year

1998-99 and M.Phil and Ph.D. programmes in the year 2009.

IGNOU followed suit and offered initially BLISc and later MLISc and Ph.D. Courses. Due to adverse reaction against starting research courses like M.Phil and Ph.D. programmes, UGC put a ban on these Courses. Later this ban was lifted allowing more Open Universities to start M.Phil and Ph.D. programmes in LIS. There are four Open Universities offering M.Phil and Ph.D. Courses in LIS. Other Open Universities may follow suit.

Conventional Universities offering LIS Courses through Distance Mode

Out of 532 Conventional Universities existing in the Country during 2009-10, only 32 Universities / Institutes were offering Courses in LIS in the Country. Some of these Universities / Institutes started Courses in distance mode before the advent of Open Universities in the Country. The following Distance Learning / Correspondence Institutes (arranged alphabetically) attached to the Conventional Universities were offering LIS Courses at different levels.

Sl. No.	Name of the University / Institution	Courses offered:
1	Alagappa University, Karaikudi (TN)	CLISc / BLISc / MLISc/PGD LAN
2	Annamalai University, Chidambaram (TN)	BLISc /MLISc / M.Phil
3	Awadesh Pratap Singh University, Rewa (MP)	BLISc
4	Barkatullah Vishwa Vidyalaya, Institute of Correspondence Courses, Bhopal (MP)	DLISc / BLISc / MLISc
5	Berhampur University, Berhampur (Odisha)	BLISc

6	Bharatidasan University, Centre for Distance Education, Trichi (TN)	MLISc
7	Birla Institute of Technology, Distance Learning Programme Division, Pilani (Rajasthan)	BLISc
8	Global Open University, Kohima (Nagaland)	BLISc / MLISc / M.Phil
9	Guru Ghasidas University, Bilaspur (Chattisgarh)	BLISc / MLISc
10	Dr.Harisingh Gour Vishwa Vidyalaya, Sagar (MP)	BLISc / MLISc
11	Institute of Advanced Studies, Dept. of Lib. & Inf.Science, Sardarsahar, District Churu (Rajasthan)	BLISc / MLISc
12	Kakatiya University, School of Distance Learning and Continuing Education (SDLCE), Warangal (AP)	CLISc / BLISc
13	Kurukshetra University, Dept. of Distance Education, Kurukshetra (Haryana)	DLISc / BLISc / MLISc
14	Kuvempu University, Directorate of Distance Education, Shimoga (Karnataka)	BLISc / MLISc
15	Lalit Narayan Mithila University, Dharbhanga (Bihar)	BLISc / MLISc
16	Maharishi Dayanand University, Rohtak (Haryana)	BLISc / MLISc
17	Madurai Kamaraj University, Institute of Correspondence Courses and Continuing Education, Madurai (TN)	CLISc /BLISc / MLISc
18	Mahatma Gandhi Gramodaya University, Chitrakoot (MP)	BLISc / MLISc
19	Mahatma Gandhi Kashi Vidya Peeth, Varanasi (UP)	BLISc
20	Mahatma Gandhi University, School of Distance Education, Kottayam (Kerala)	BLISc
21	Mohanlal Sukhadia University, Udaipur (Rajasthan)	CLISc
22	National Open School, New Delhi	CLISc

23	North Orissa University, Baripada, Odisha	BLISc
24	Punjabi University, Dept. of Correspondence Courses, Patiala (Punjab)	DLISc / BLISc / MLISc
25	Patna University, Directorate of Distance Education, Patna (Bihar)	BLISc
26	Sri Venkateshwara University, Institute of Correspondence Courses, Tirupati (AP)	BLISc
27	University of Calicut, School of Distance Education, Calicut (Kerala)	BLISc
28	University of Hyderabad, Hyderabad (AP)	PGD LAN
29	University of Kashmir, Department of Distance Education, Srinagar (J&K)	CLISc
30	University of Madras, Institute of Correspondence Education, Chennai (TN)	CLISc / BLISc / MLISc
31	University of Rajasthan, Jaipur (Rajasthan)	CLISc
32	Vinayaka Mission University, Salem (TN)	CLISc / BLISc / PGD LAN / M.Phil

The Report on UGC Model Curriculum: Library and Information Science identified the following Universities / Institutions offering LIS Education Programmes through Correspondence / Distance mode in India.

Sl. No.	Name of the University	Courses	Minimum Qualifications	Mode
1	Indira Gandhi National Open University, New Delhi	BLIS, MLIS	Graduate BLIS	DE
2	Dr.B.R.Ambedkar Open University, Hyderabad.	BLIS, MLIS	GraduateBLIS	DE
3	Yeswant Rao Chavan Maharashtra Open University, Nasik	BLIS	Graduate	DE

4	Birla Institute of Technology and Science, Pilani	Info.Sc./Systems	—	NA
5	Kakatiya University, Warangal	CLIS, BLISc	Intermediate Graduate + ET	DE
6	Sri Venkateshwara University, Tirupati	CLIS, BLIS	Intermediate Graduate	Formal/ DE
7	Barkhatulla Vishwa Vidyalaya, Bhopal	DLIS, BLISc MLIS	Hr.Secondary Graduate BLIS	DE
8	Kota Open University, Kota	DLIS, Ph.D.	Hi.Secondary MLIS 50%	DE
9	University of Calicut, Calicut	BLIS	Graduate 45% PG	DE
10	University of Madras, Chennai	CLIS, BLIS MLIS	Sr.Secondary Graduate BLIS	DE / Formal
11	Awdesh Pratap Singh University, Rewa	BLIS	Graduate 45%	DE
12	Kurukshetra University, Kurukshetra	DLIS	Hr.Secondary	Formal/ DE
13	Patna University, Patna	BLISc	Graduate	Formal/ DE
14	Guru Ghasidas University, Bilaspur	MLIS	BLIS	Formal/ DE
15	Annamalai University, Annamalainagar (TN)	BLISc MLIS	Graduate BLIS	Formal/ DE
16	Alagappa University, Karaikudi	BLIS	Graduate	DE
17	Bharatidasan University, Tiruchirapalli	BLIS	Graduate	DE
18	Mahatma Gandhi Gramodaya Vishwavidyalaya, Chitrakoot	BLIS	Graduate	DE
19	University of Kashmir, Srinagar	CLIS	Matriculatyion	Formal/ DE
20	Madurai Kamaraj University, Madurai	CLIS, BLISc	Matriculation Graduate	DE
21	Nalanda University, Patna	DLIS, BLIS	Intermediate Graduate	DE

22 Panjabi University, Patiala	DLIS	Matriculation with English 50%	Formal/ DE
23 Dr. Harisingh Gour Vishwa Vidyalaya, Sagar	BLIS, MLIS	Graduate BLIS	DE
24 Jai Narain Vyas University Omkarmalsomani College, Jodhpur	CLIS	Sr.Hr.Secondary with 40%	
25 University of Hyderabad, Hyderabad	PGD LAN	BLIS	DE
26 Lalit Narayan Mithila University, Darbhanga	BLIS MLIS	Graduate BLIS	DE

Source: UGC Model Curriculum: Library and Information Science, New Delhi, UGC, 2001. Appendix-III. Pp.146-147.

The proliferation of Courses through distance modes had a negative effect on the quality of LIS education in the Country. The quality of the products specially turned out by Institutes of Correspondence / distance education attached to traditional Universities is questionable. The main purpose of these institutions is to spin money by admitting hundreds of distance learners, if not, in thousands. The Course material produced by these Institutes is substandard and not learner friendly. Some of the course material is not revised frequently to include latest developments in the subjects concerned. Every year hundreds of so called 'qualified' candidates flood the employment market for jobs and thereby coming in the way genuinely qualified candidates. This type of proliferation of candidates indirectly effects the quality of services offered by the Library and Information Centres in the Country. With the exception of few Correspondence Course Institutes, in most of the Institutes, the courses offered are below accepted norms and standards.

The candidates who obtain degrees in LIS through distance mode are flooding the employment market and competing with the candidates who came through regular courses offered by the traditional universities in the country. V.K.J. Jeevan aptly opined that "the staunch supporters and facilitators of distance education should conduct proper surveys and initiate professional courses via distance mode only when there is a demand far exceeding the supply through the higher stream"[6].

REFERENCES

1. Peters, O. Theoretical aspects of Correspondence instruction. *In* O.Mackenzie and E. L. Christensen, *Eds. The Changing world of Correspondence Study.* University Park, Pensylvania State (USA), 1971. Pp.27-32.
2. Rai, Pradeep. Library and Information Science Education through distance mode in India. *In Dynamics of Librarianship in the Knowledge Society.* V4. *Ed.* by D. Chandran, *etal.* Delhi, B. R. Publishing Corporation, 2012. Pp.1278-1288.\
3. Prakash, P and Krishna Rao, P. Issues in Open and Distance Education. *University News,* V50, N27, July 02-08, 2012. Pp.11-19.
4. Basu, Swaraj and Sri Vatsav, Manjulika. Look beyond conventional wisdom: Need for National Policy on ODL. *University News,* V50, N27, July 02-08, 2012. Pp.11-19.
5. Rai, Pradeep. Library and Information Science Education through distance mode in India. *Opcit.* Pp.1278-1288.
6. Jeevan, V.K.J. Education for Library and Information Science on the distance mode in India: A critique. Librarian Career Development. V7, N2, 1999. P.14.

5

Committees on Curriculum Development

Webster's Dictionary defines Curriculum "1. as Courses offered by an education institution or one of its branches. 2. A set of Courses". Chambers Dictionary defines it as "a Course especially the course of study at a University". On the other hand syllabus means a summary outline of a discourse; treatise or course of study or of examination requirements. Generally these two words Curriculum and Syllabus is used synonymously and the difference between these two words is very thin. In its broadest sense a Curriculum may be refer to all courses offered at a 'school'. A curriculum may also refer to a defined and prescribed course of studies which students must fulfill in order to pass a certain level of education in the Schools, Colleges, Universities and other higher educational Institutions.

In the field of Library and Information Science which has hundred years of history, the curriculum has gone several changes keeping in view of the needs of changing times to turn out quality products to manage the Library and Information Centres in the

Country effectively. In this regard several Commissions and Committees have been appointed by the University Grants Commission (UGC) to look in to the existing Curriculum / Syllabus being taught in the University Library Schools / Departments and suggest suitable Curriculum / Syllabus so as to bring quality in LIS Education and to bring out well trained manpower so as to meet the requirements of Library and Information Centres in the Country. In the following paras an attempt has been made to present briefly important recommendations made by the committees appointed mainly by the UGC and other Agencies.

5.1. RANGANATHAN COMMITTEE ON UNIVERSITY AND COLLEGE LIBRARIES (1957)

The UGC appointed a Committee in 1957 under the Chairmanship of Dr. S. R. Ranganatghan, to advise the Commission "on matters relating to the proper functioning and management of libraries. In the year 1959, the UGC conducted a Seminar titled "From Publisher to Reader" held on March 4-7, 1959 at Vigyan Bhavan, New Delhi. The Report of the Library Committee and proceedings of the Seminar was published by the UGC under the title "*University and College Libraries*" in the year 1965.

The Report mostly deals with the various aspects of University and College Libraries in India. In Chapter L: Training of Library Personnel, the Committee emphasized the need for quality library training to provide professional leadership. It also dealt with levels of training viz; Semi Professional, professional and training in research. The Committee opined that the Certificate Course in Library Science should be left to the care of Departments of Libraries and Library Association of each State.

It categorized Departments of Library Science as first grade and second grade departments. It stated that only first grade departments in the universities should conduct B.Lib.Sc. / M.Lib.Sc courses. The second grade departments maintained by the universities should offer only a PG Courses leading to the award of B.Lib.Sc degree. The Report also specifies the qualifications for Professor, Reader, Lecturer and Demonstrator including teachers' strength in the First and Second Grade Departments, Teacher-Student Ratio, provision of research facility in the First Grade Department and minimum qualifications for admission to B.Lib.Sc/ M.Lib.Sc Courses.

In Chapter P under Summary of Chief Recommendations, the Committee under the heading "Department of Library Science" recommended that First Grade Department of Library Science may conduct Courses for B.Lib.Sc and M.Lib.Sc and a Second Grade only for B.Lib.Sc and semi-professional Course should be left over to Library Associations. The Committee also recommended that a First Grade Department of LIS should have one Professor, one Reader, two Lecturers and also Demonstrators. In the case of Second Grade Department, it should have one Reader, one Lecturer and one Demonstrator. Under 'Course of Studies in Library Science' the Committee recommended that 'only a graduate should be admitted to B.Lib.Sc Course'. It further specified that "a person should be allowed to join the B.Lib.Sc Course only after the satisfactory completion of an apprentice course of six months in a Library approved for the purpose". It further recommended that "a Committee of Experts should be appointed by Commission to examine the question of improving and coordinating the standards of teaching and research in the Departments of Library

Science of the Universities and to give advice on the Courses of Studies, Standards and Teaching[1].

The Committee has not recommended model curricula for B.Lib.Sc / M.Lib.Sc Courses conducted by the Universities in the Country. This aspect was left to another Committee headed by Dr. S. R. Ranganahan and appointed by the UGC. The Report was published by the UGC in 1965 under the title "Library Science in Indian Universities"[2]. Nevertheless Ranganathan Committee on University and College Libraries serving as a basic document on matters relating to State of Affairs of University and College Libraries in Indian during the 1960s. Much water has been flown under the bridge since then, but some of the basic recommendations on University and College Libraries hold good even today with minor modifications. Many of the Academic Libraries in the Country were not able to come near to the recommendations of the Committee even after five decades.

5.2. REPORT OF ADVISORY COMMITTEE FOR LIBRARIES (1958)

This Committee was appointed by the Ministry of Education, Government of India in the year 1958 under the Chairmanship of K.P. Sinha to look into the 'state of Libraries in India'. In one of terms of reference it was stated "to go into the question of the training of librarians and conditions of their service". The report of the Committee under Chapter-7: 'Training for Librarianship' dealt in a detailed manner aspects such as: Training of semi professional staff, Training of Professional Librarians and discussed the Courses to be offered at semiprofessional and professional levels. In one of the recommendations with regards to

University level courses it made the following recommendations. "The University Grants Commission should strengthen the existing diploma courses in the first instance in order to enable the universities running classes in Library Science to create separate Departments of Library Education and give adequate financial assistance to the universities for this purpose". In another recommendation it was stated that "some of the Universities should also provide advanced courses in Librarianship, leading to M.A., Degree in Librarianship". The Committee also recommended that "Universities should also encourage research in Librarianship. Special funds should be provided for this purpose"[3].

Subjects listed for Diploma Course in Librarianship

The following subjects have been listed for offering Diploma in Librarianship at the University level.

1. Classification Theory
2. Classification Practice
3. Cataloguing Theory
4. Cataloguing Practice
5. Bibliography
6. Reference Works
7. Book Selection
8. Organization and Administration
9. Cultural History of India and General Knowledge
10. Preservation of Books and Records
11. Evaluation and Development of Writing Books and Libraries, and
12. Language.

The Course Contents for Papers 1 – 8 were briefly presented under Chapter VII[4].

This Report primarily deals with the development of libraries in the country, with special reference to Public Libraries. Nevertheless it also turned its attention to training for librarianship and dealt with the Courses such as Semi-professional and Professional levels and made suitable recommendations in this regard. This was one of the oldest Committee Reports which turned its attention to LIS Education before the Dr. S. Ranganathan Committee appointed by the UGC in 1965. A sea change has taken place in LIS education scenario in the country since 1959.

5.3. REPORT OF THE UNIVERSITY GRANTS COMMISSION (UGC) REVIEW COMMITTEE (1965)

The Committee was appointed by the UGC in 1965 under the Chairmanship of Dr. S. R. Ranganathan, 'to review the standards of teaching and research in Library Science in Indian Universities'. The Report was published under the title *"Library Science in Indian Universities"* in 965 by the UGC[5]. The Report was presented in five chapters viz: *1. Introduction, 2. Existing Facilities of Teaching and Research, 3. Syllabus, 4. Sectors for Research in Library Science and 5. Recommendation with two appendixes.* Appendix-II consists of several statements numbering 20 based on the summary of replies to the questionnaire regarding facilities for teaching and research in Library Science in Indian Universities.

Major Recommendations of the Review Committee

The Review Committee in its report traced the then existing facilities of teaching and research and suggested syllabi for CLSc, BLISc and MLISc programmes and identified sectors for research in Library Science. It has also made far reaching recommendations covering aspects such as: minimum qualifications for admission to courses, pre-admission courses, university courses such as Ph.D., M.Lib.Sc and B.Lib.Sc, methods of teaching and relative place of theory and practices, equivalence of Diploma in Library Science and B .Lib.Sc, non-professional subjects in the LIS curriculum, examination, working hours, minimum qualifications for LIS teachers, staff requirement, physical facilities, books, training of teachers, research, survey of trained personnel – needs and quality and cooperation between the Departments of Library Science and the Library.

For nearly three decades the said report has served as *Bible* or basic document for drafting syllabi for individual Library Schools in the Country to meet their local requirements. Majority of the Library Schools followed the syllabus suggested by the Review Committee with minor changes even though some of the topics suggested by the Committee have lost the relevance due to advent of Information and Communication Technologies on the scene.

Many of the recommendations of the Committee remained only on paper and majority of the LIS Departments were not able to implement them and there by producing substandard products to manage libraries and information centres in the Country. The Report of the Committee slowly lost its relevance due to changes taking place in the arena of LIS in the country. Its importance or relevance was felt only during the seminars, conferences at the local, regional or national levels and used for tracing the history of LIS Curriculum in the Country.

Syllabi suggested by the Review Committee

After stating the objectives of each Course, the

Committee identified detailed Course Contents under each paper to be offered at CLSc, B.Lib.Sc and M.Lib.Sc levels. For CLSc which is a semi-professional course not offered by the Universities, the Committee suggested the following Scheme of Papers.

1. Library Routine
2. Library Service and Organisation
3. Library Cataloguing
4. Record of Practical Work

The following is the Scheme of Papers recommended for B.Lib.Sc. Course:

1. Library Organisation
2. Library Administration
3. Physical Bibliography and Book Selection
4. Document Bibliography and Reference Service
5. Library Classification (Theory)
6. Library Classification (Practice)
7. Library Catalogue (Theory)
8. Library Catalogue (Practice)
9. Record and Practical Work

The following is the Scheme of Papers recommended for M.Lib.Sc. Course:

1. Universe of Knowledge, its development and structure
2. Depth Classification (Theory)
3. Depth Classification (Practice)
4. Advanced Library Catalogue
5. Any one of the following:
    a) Public Library System
    b) Academic Library System
    c) Research and Technical Library System

   d) Documentation
6. Project during term time; and
7. Literature Survey in any one of the following fields:
   a) Indology
   b) A Subject in Humanities
   c) A Subject in Social Sciences
   d) One of the Applied Sciences
   e) Government Documents
   f) Juvenile Literature

Changes in the LIS Curriculum

For nearly two decades i.e. until 1980s most of the LIS Departments in the Country to a greater extent, with minor changes, followed the model syllabus recommended by the Review Committee. After 1980s we could notice a marked change in the curriculum of BLISc / MLISc Courses due to changes in the information scenario of the Country and the emergence of Information and Communication Technologies and slow adoption of Information Technologies (IT) in Libraries and Information Centres. The emphasis which was laid on Physical and Document Bibliography in BLISc Course gave place to Reference and Information Sources and Services. Library Organization has been replaced by Library and Society (or Community). The emphasis on Classification and Cataloguing (Theory and Practice) has been drastically reduced, if not completely eliminated. Library Administration has been replaced by Library Management. In few Library Science Schools / Departments a beginning has been made to introduce a paper on 'Computer Applications' in BLISc Curriculum.

Changes in MLISc Curriculum

The Msters Degree Programme has under gone significant changes as result of the advent of Information and Communication Technologies (ICT). Most of the LIS Schools have dropped the Paper on 'Universe of Knowledge', which was the brain child of Dr. S. R. Ranganathan, and reduced undue emphasis given to Advanced Classification and Cataloguing (Theory and Practice). The electives hither to occupied a prominent place in LIS Curriculum have also been dropped, with few exceptions. Some of the LIS Schools even dropped 'Project Work' and 'Literature Survey' due to obvious reasons of usefulness and practicality and / or practicability. To a larger extent the present MLISc curricula include new areas such as: Information and Communication; Information Systems and Programmes (or Services); Information Technology; Computer Applications in Libraries; Resource Sharing and Networking; Bibliographic Databases and Networks and Research Methods in LIS. Of late Digital Library, Resources and Management, Library Software has been given due place in the LIS Curriculum. The Review Committee has not given due thought to M.Phil programme, even though it has made specific recommendations for Ph.D. programmes.

5.4. ANDHRA PRADESH PUBLIC LIBRARIES ACT, 1960 REVIEW COMMITTEE (1976) (EKBOTE COMMITTEE)

The Government of Andhra Pradesh through its G.O. Ms. No. 198, dated February 25, 1976 appointed A. P. Public Libraries Act Review Committee[6] to go into the working of A. P. Public Libraries Act, 1960 and the administration of Public Libraries in Andhra Pradesh and suggest amendments to the existing provision in the Act under the Chairmanship of Justice Gopal Rao Ekbote, former Chief Justice of Andhra Pradesh High Court with 13 Members. It is popularly known as 'Ekbote Committee Report'.

The Committee submitted its report in the year 1978. It is a voluminous report consisting 14 Chapters with 13 Appendices. In one of the Chapters (XII) the Committee dealt on LIS Education in Andhra Pradesh. The Committee with regards to degree course in LIS observed that "all the three Universities in our State, that is to say Osmania, Andhra and Sri Venkateshwara Universities have arrangements for degree Courses". The Committee concentrated its thoughts on the conducting of Certificate Course in Library Science to turn out semi professions. It made a number of recommendations in this regard. Some of them are as follows.

1. There should be a library training course for training of library technicians in the Course known as Certificate Course. There should be arrangement for in-service training for librarians.
2. The basic general qualification for admission to this Course should not be lower than a first or second class pass in Intermediate or Junior College.
3. The duration of the Course should not be less than 150 working days of five hours a day each hour being 60 minutes.
4. The Government should constitute a small but effective Committee of Experts to draft Syllabus for a) Library Course, b) Teachers Training for Teachers who teach in the Schools, c) In-service Training of the Librarians as well as teachers.

5. There should be uniform syllabus, duration of period and examination, etc., for the Course run by the Association or Department.
6. In the training of Librarians for Public Libraries, a Course in Adult Education Administration and Techniques should be added. Similarly Library Administration and Library Extension Methods should form part of Training of Adult Education Workers.
7. More Text Books and other books on Library Science should be written in Telugu or translated from foreign languages...
8. The teachers in Library School should take tutorials; adopt Seminar and Discussion Method of Teaching rather than relying only on lectures. Case Study Method should also be followed.
9. Teachers should know new methodology of teaching and if necessary undergo training for that purpose.
10. At least part of the teaching staff in Library Science School should be full time. (Pp.107-108).

Course Contents

The Committee has not made any specific recommendation with regards to Course Contents for CLSc Course. In the course of its observations it opined that "the instruction is build up around these traditional disciplines such as cataloguing, classification, reference and bibliography, administration, the history of books and history of libraries. Apart from these, the general subject concerning the theory or introduction to librarianship and the book selection" (P.90).

Institutions conducting Semi-professional Courses in Andhra Pradesh:

1. Institute of Library Science (1953), Hyderabad.
2. Paturi Nagabhusanam School of Library Science (1966) of APLA, Vijayawada.
3. Vavilala School of Library Science (1994), Guntur.
4. Rayalaseema Institute of Library Science (1989), Kadapa.
5. Gnanasai Library Institute, Jadcherla (Mahaboobnagar District).
6. Naveen Vivekananda College of Library Science, Hyderabad.
7. State Institute of Library Education, Research and Training (SILERT) (A Division of Director of Public Libraries, Govt. of Andhra Pradesh).

These Courses were recognized by the Government of Andhra Pradesh. The Commissioner of Examinations, Govt. of Andhra Pradesh conducts the examinations and awards certificates. The above seven Institutions follow the common syllabus approved by the committee constituted by the Director of Public Libraries, Govt. of Andhra Pradesh. The Syllabus is as follows:

Paper	Subject	Marks
I	Library Classification and Cataloguing (Theory)	100
II	Library Classification (Practice)	100
III	Library Cataloguing (Practice)	100
IV	Library Administration and Organisation	100
V	Reference Service, Bibliography and Book Selection	100
VI	Internal Assessment.	100

5.5. UGC PANEL ON LIBRARY AND INFORMATION SCIENCE (1981)

UGC, the body which looks after the affairs of higher education in the country constituted Subject

Panels for various Subject Fields in Sciences, Social Sciences and Humanities. It has also constituted Subject Panel in the field of Library and Information Science with the following terms of reference.

1. To advise on measures for enhancing the quality of work in teaching and research and make recommendations in this connection to the Commission.
2. To prepare periodically status reports regarding research facilities, research areas, performances and perspectives and indicate areas of thrust and importance and suggest measures to improve quality.
3. To render advice on such other matters as may be referred to them by the Commission[7]. (These subject Panels have been abolished in the year 2000)

The UGC Panel on Library and Information Science at its meeting held on September 19, 1981 formulated syllabi for BLISc / MLISc / M.Phil programmes and in addition formulated in respect of: *a) Strength of the Faculty, b) Qualifications for Teachers, c) Establishing and Strengthening a Department*[8].

The Panel also while appreciating the usefulness of (the then) existing Pattern of Bachelor's and Master's Degree Courses in LIS at the PG level, also recognized the need for two year integrated programme in LIS. The recommendations of the LIS Panel were accepted by the UGC and circulated them to LIS Schools / Departments in the Country in January and March 1982 for guidance and observation. The Panel also identified the objectives of BLISc, MLISc, M.Phil and Ph.D. programmes and identified the following Curriculum for each of these courses except Ph.D. Programme.

The Papers for BLISc Course included the following:

1. Library and Society
2. Library Classification (Theory)
3. Library Classification (Practice)
4. Library Cataloguing and Subject Indexing (Theory)
5. Library Cataloguing and Subject Indexing (Practice)
6. Reference and Information Sources
7. Reference and Information Services, and
8. Library Management and Administration

The Master's Degree Programme includes the following Papers:

1. Universe of Knowledge
2. One of the following:
   a) Information Storage and Retrieval
   b) Depth Classification
3. Information Systems and Programmes
4. Information and Literature Sources in any of the following:
   a) Humanities
   b) Social Sciences
   c) Sciences
   d) Medical Science
   e) Engineering and Technology
   f) Agricultural Science, etc.
5. One of the following:
   a) Computer Applications in Libraries / Information Centres
   b) Comparative Librarianship

   c) LIS Education
6. Operations Research and Systems Analysis
7. One of the following:
   a) Public Library System
   b) Academic Library System
   c) Research and Technical Library System
   d) Agriculture Library System
   e) Medical Library System
   f) Engineering and Technological Library System, and
8. Project and Dissertation

The Curriculum for M.Phil programme consists of two parts. **Part-I** consists of three papers: viz: *1. Research Methods, 2. Library Planning and Management and 3. Any of the following Options: a) University and College Library System, b) Research and Technical Library System, c) Public Library System, d) Information processing and Organization, e) Information transfer and Dissemination, f) Comparative Librarianship and g) Education for LIS.* **Part-II**: Dissertation. As regards Ph.D. programme the Panel recommendation states that "Original research and theoretical and applied on any aspects of Library Science with a view to extending the knowledge boundaries of the discipline"[9].

Influence of Review Committee

The UGC Panel on Library and Information science could not come out of the influence of the Review Committee as the former retained some of the papers suggested by later even after nearly two decades. In BLISc Programme the emphasis given to Library Classification and Cataloguing (Theory and Practice) by the Review Committee has been retained by the UGC Panel. Library Organization and Library Administration (Papers 1 and 2) suggested by the Review Committee have been clubbed and re-designated as Library Management and Administration (Paper-8) by the UGC Panel. Physical Bibliography and Document Bibliography (Papers 3 & 4) suggested by the Review Committee have been replaced by two papers viz: Reference and Information Sources and Services (Papers 6 and 7) by the UGC Panel. The Papers recommended for MLISc Programme by the UGC Panel underwent few changes and modifications when compared with the papers recommended by the Review Committee. The UGC Panel retained Universe of Knowledge (Paper-1). Depth Classification and Advanced Library Catalogue (Theory and Practice) suggested by the Review Committee has been partially dropped by the UGC Panel and retained it as one of the electives under Paper-II "One of the following". The UGC Panel included two new papers titled *Information Systems and Programmes (Paper-III)* and *Operations Research and Systems Analysis (Paper-VI)*. The Paper on *Literature Survey (Paper-III)* suggested by the Review Committee has been retained in the Syllabus suggested by the UGC Panel as *Paper-IV: "Information and Literature Source in any one of the following"*. The Electives suggested by the Review Committee under Paper-V were retained by the UGC Panel under Paper-VII: *One of the following"*. The Project Report finds a place in both the model syllalbi under Paper-IV (Review Committee) and under Paper-VIII) (UGC Panel).

In addition, the UGC Panel included one more elective under Paper-V: One of the following: a) Computer Applications, b) Comparative Librarianship and c) LIS Education. The two groups of electives suggested by the UGC Panel for MLISc Course also find a place in the curriculum suggested for M.Phil programme under Part-I, Paper-III (Any of the following Options). It appears that different library systems such as Public, Academic, Research and Technical have greater influence and impact in the then contemporary LIS Education in the Country and therefore the persons who drafted the LIS Curriculum dared not to drop them even though the concept of different library systems have undergone radical changes in due course of time and in the present information scenario where the boundaries between different library systems have been fast vanishing after the advent of ICT and emergence of resource sharing and networking[10].

5.6. REPORT OF THE CURRICULUM DEVELOPMENT COMMITTEE (CDC) ON LIS (1990)

The UGC in September 1990 appointed Curriculum Development Committee (CDC) to restructure the courses of studies in LIS under the Chairmanship of Prof. P. N.Kaula. The Committee submitted its report and it was published by the UGC in September 1992[11]. The Committee identified objectives of courses such as BLISc, MLISc, MLISc (Integrated), M.Phil and P.D. The six core papers for BLISc include:

1. Library and Information Society;
2. Library and Information Management;
3. Library Classification (Theory and Practice);
4. Library Cataloging and Subject Indexing (Theory and Practice);
5. Information Sources and Services; and
6. Computer Applications.

It has identified sixteen elective papers for BLISc Programme which appears rather strange. And also it was doubtful whether the required expertise was available in the LIS Departments to teach these elective papers. Generally electives are included in the curriculum for MLISc Courses. These elective include:

1. School and Children's Libraries;
2. University and College Libraries;
3. Public Library System;
4. Government Department Libraries;
5. Research and Development Libraries;
6. Archives Librarianship;
7. Engineering and Technology Library and Information System;
8. Medical Librarianship;
9. Agricultural Library and Information System
10. Law Libraries;
11. Music Libraries;
12. Industrial Library and Information System;
13. Manuscriptology;
14. Library Buildings, Fittings and Furniture;
15. Local Studies Librarianship; and
16. Non-Book Materials

The Curriculum for MLISc (one year programme) consists of both core and elective e papers. The five core papers include: *1. Information and Communication: Evolution and Development; 2. Library and Information Management, Sources and Services; 3. Computer Technology, Library Automation and Information System; 4. Information Processing and Retrieval; and 5. Research Methodology and Informetrics.*

The elective paper for MLISc (one year) programme include: *1. Comparative and International Librarianship; 2. Higher Education and Academic Library System; 3.*

Communication, Mass Media and Public Library; 4. Bibliographic Control; 5. User Education and 6. Education for Library and Information Science.

MLISc Two Year Programme (Integrated Course)

The MLISc (Two Year Integrated Programme) Course consists of five core papers for the first year and four core papers for the second year and also two groups of optional papers. Each group consists of ten papers of which a candidate shall have to opt for two electives in the previous year and two in the final year i.e. one each from Group-A and B for each year.

The first year core papers include: *1. Foundations of Librarianship; 2. Library and Information Management; 3. Library Classification — Theory and Practice; 4. Library Cataloguing and Indexing – Theory and Practice; 5. Information Sources and Services.*

The second year core papers include: *1. Information and Communication: Evolution and Development; 2. Information Processing and Retrieval; 3. Computer Applications, Library Automation and Information Systems; 4. Research Methodology and Informetrics.*

Optional Papers in Group-A

1. Higher Education and Academic Library System;
2. Communication, Mass Media and Public Library System;
3. School and Children's Libraries;
4. Medical Libraries;
5. Law Libraries;
6. Music Libraries;
7. Engineering and Technology Libraries;
8. Agricultural Libraries;

9. Industrial Libraries; and
10. Archive Libraries.

Optional Papers in Group-B

1. Bibliographic Control;
2. Education for LIS;
3. User Studies and User Education;
4. Comparative and International Librarianship;
5. Manuscriptlogy;
6. Preservation and Conservation;
7. Learning Skills and Reading Habits;
8. Library Buildings;
9. Local Studies Librarianship; and
10. Non-book Materials.

M.Phil and Ph.D. Programmes

The CDC Report suggested four Papers for M.Phil Programme. These include:

1. Research Methodology;
2. Current Trends in Library and Information Science;
3. Literature Survey; and
4. Dissertation and Viva-voce.

The main objectives of this M.Phil programme is to identify problem areas and apply methods of research and design experiments to find solutions to the problems and to formulate research problems and to effectively present projects and / or dissertations.

The CDC Report also stated the objectives of Ph.D. Programme and identified some of the areas related to L IS. The two objectives stated are:

1. To undertake research work independently and

2. To give specialized knowledge in-depth on any topic related to LIS, allied subjects and inter-disciplinary areas.

The broad areas identified for carrying out research are:

1. Structure and Development of Knowledge;
2. Classification, Cataloging and Indexing;
3. Information Studies;
4. Computer Applications;
5. Historical Studies in Library and Allied Subjects;
6. Social and Economic Aspects of Librarianship;
7. Library and Information Management and Systems Analysis;
8. Application of techniques of Library and Information Science to evaluate other disciplines; and other allied relevant themes.

Other Aspects

In addition, CDC Report lists out a number of special courses, about 40, on recent advances in LIS to supplement and compliment BLISc and MLISc courses. It has also suggested Orientation Programmes for teachers of LIS to keep them abreast of new developments in the field of LIS. It has also suggested an action plan for organizing such orientation programmes of four to five weeks duration.

Reactions and Comments on CDC Report

There had been adverse reactions and comments on CDC Report. The teaching Community by and large has not favorably reacted to the said Report. The Report failed to take into consideration ground realities obtaining in the LIS Departments in the Country. There has been overlapping of Courses suggested for BLISc,

MLISc and MLISc (two-year integrated) programmes. The number of Optionals / Electives suggested for these programs is baffling and one wonders whether the required expertise and infrastructure, library facilities were available in the LIS Departments in the Country. The books recommended for each course was devoid of full bibliographical details. The Committee was choosy in selecting the so called Experts / Resource Persons which it has consulted and invited 'its own people' for participation in the workshops held on 12th February 1991. In the opinion of some critics, the Committee failed to undertake critical review of the existing curricula / syllabi and courses of study offered at different levels and regions of the Country and suggest appropriate and suitable measures for modernizing and restructuring into Unit Courses. The Report failed to make LIS Education more meaningful and reflect the needs and aspirations of its beneficiaries as well as to make it more relevant to changing information scenario in the Country. The List of books recommended at the end of each Course was awfully presented with overlaps and bibliographical errors. It was almost a dead Report for all practical purposes[12].

5.7. UNESCO (PGI) MODULAR CURRICULUM

The UNESCO (PGI) has circulated "A Modular Curriculum in Information Studies" prepared by J.A. Large in 1987 for the benefit of the Member States[13]. This Document was intended as a basic resource from which Curricula can be designed / or constructed by individual LIS Schools to meet the local needs and requirements. The said document listed twelve core modules as well as eight elective modules. The titles of core modules include:

1. Information in its Social and Communication Context;
2. Information Users;
3. Quantitative Methods;
4. Research Methods;
5. Information Sources;
6. Information Storage and Retrieval Systems;
7. Information Services;
8. Electronic Data Processing;
9. Application Information Technology;
10. Tele-Communications and Networking in Information Systems and Services;
11. Management of Information Systems and Services;
12. Economics and Marketing of Information.

The titles of Elective Modules include:

1. Design of Computer assisted information systems;
2. Sectoral / Subject Oriented Information Sources and Systems;
3. Planning and design of buildings and facilities for Information Centres and Libraries;
4. Online Searching;
5. Health and Welfare Library and Information Services;
6. Agricultural Library and Information Services;
7. Audio-visual Studies;
8. Printing, book binding and conservation.

The said document also provides for titles of other possible elective modules at Page 74.

Impact of Modular Curriculum

The Modular Curriculum circulated by PGI (UNESCO) had some impact on the Curricula of courses offered by Indian Library Schools. Many LIS Schools have included some of the modules, with some modifications, in their curricula especially for Master's Degree Programmes. This document to some extent reflects the needs of LIS School in the developing countries. Some of the modules listed in the UNESCO (PGI) Document find a place in the CDC Report with some modifications.

5.8. UGC MODEL CURRICULUM: LIBRARY AND INFORMATION SCIENCE (1998)

UGC's Fresh Initiative

The CDC Report was not given enough thought and a chance for its implementation if not in toto, but partially by the LIS Departments in the Country. Fresh initiative was taken by the UGC Panel on LIS which was reconstituted the Subject Panel in LIS 1997 with Prof. C. R. Karisiddappa as its Convener. The General Terms of Reference among other things included preparation of status report and also modification of existing guidelines.

The Subject Panel on LIS took up the work of preparation of the new CDC Report at its first meeting held in Karnatak University, Dharwad on 10 – 11 March, 1998. The modus operandi for the preparation of status report and model syllabus in LIS was discussed in a couple of meetings of the Panel. On further advice from the UGC, the Subject Panel Members interacted with the 'Conveners' (Chair Persons) of BOS in LIS of various Universities in the Country by conducting four zonal meetings which were held at Kurukshetra University (12-13 November, 1998), Utkal University (09-10 December, 1998), Osmania University (29-30 December 1998) and North Eastern Hill Universities (13-14 April, 1999). The Panel also circulated a questionnaire to all the LIS Departments in the Country to elicit more information for the preparation of Status Report.

The UGC issued fresh directions for the preparation of CDC Report on March 8, 2000 and August 31, 2000 wherein it was advised to constitute three groups consisting eight members each for completing the work of preparation of CDC Report. These three Groups met in UGC Office on 23rd to 25th October 2000, 4th 6th December, 2000 and 8th to 10th January 2001 respectively and finalized the Levels, Modules, Model Syllabus, Marks Pattern, Teaching Hours and Credits. The said Report was released under the title ***"UGC Model Curriculum: Library and Information Science"*** [14].

The Report[15] consists of 2 Parts. In Part-I, we find A) Introduction; A.1) The Discipline of LIS; A.2) Land Marks in LIS Education; A.3) Status of LIS Education; A.4) UGC Efforts towards LIS Education and Curriculum Development; A.5) Guiding Factors; A.6) Summing up and A.7) Summary of Recommendations. Under this section we find Course Pattern (A.7.1), Curricular Structure (A.7.2), Infrastructure (A.7.3) and Distance Education (A.7.4).

Under Section-B (Part-I) we find Level and Modules for LIS Education. In sub-section B.1 we find Introduction to Levels and Modules. In B.2 we find Detailed Modules. In section C: Model Syllabus (MLISc Integrated) has been presented. In Section-D: other Areas of concern were presented which include: Allotment of Marks and Teaching Hours (D.1), Breakup of allotted Study Hours (D.2), Infrastructure Facilities Development (D.3). In Section E: Distance Education in LIS: Norms and Standards which deals with: Status (E.1) and Norms and Standards (E.2).

In Part-II Section F: deals with Status Report on LIS Education. At the end we find four Annexures.

Modular Approach

Prof. Karisiddappa Committee adopted Mudular Approach as suggested by J. A. Large in 1982 and Dr. Vasant Gowrikar in 1998 so that the Departments of Library and Information Science in the Country to adopt the Curriculum as per their needs and requirements. The Committee prepared 6 Core Modules and 1 Module on Electives which were as follows:

Module-1: Foundations of Library and Information Science.

Module-2: Knowledge Organisation, Information Processing and Retrieval.

Module-3: Information Sources, Products and Services.

Module-4: Management of Library and Information Centres / Institutions.

Module-5: Information Technology: Basics and Applications.

Module-6: Research Methods and Statistical Techniques.

Module-7: Electives: Information Systems.

The following is the conceptual structure viz:

1. Course Objectives
2. Unit wise Course Content
3. Special note on Practical Component and
4. Learning outcome of each model was adopted to present the Modules.

The Committee hoped that "the Modules might be adopted to any one of the education patterns, viz: two Years Integrated MLISc, one year each of BLISc and MLISc, or two year integrated MLISc (Semester Scheme)". For the seven Core Modules (6 + 1) a detailed syllabus was presented between the Pages 17 and 32 with objectives and learning outcome of each module. Between Pages 35 and 47 a detailed model syllabus for Master of Library and Information Science (2-year Integrated Course) was presented.

At Page 48 of the Report, the Committee under the heading "Other Areas of Concern" presented: 1. Allotment of Marks and teaching Hours and 2. Breakup of allotted Study Hours. As an example, allotment of marks and teaching hours and breakup of allotted study hours was present to MLISc (Integrated / Semester System) at Pages 48 and 49.

Under Infrastructure Facilities Development (D.3), the Committee recommended for Training of Teachers (D.3.1) and establishment of IT Laboratory in Departments (D.3.2).

For MLISc Course (Integrated / Semester) Semester I & II, MLISc I year, the Committee recommended the following Papers including allotment of Marks and hours of teaching programme.

Paper No.	Paper Title:	Th	IA/PR	Exam Marks	Total Marks	Hours
1	Fundamentals of Library and Information Science	—	—	100	100	120
2	Knowledge Organisqtion, Information Processing and Retrieval (Th)	—	—	100	100	120
3	Knowledge Organisation, Information Processing and Retrieval (Pr)	—	—	—	100	120
	i) Document Cataloguing	—	50	50		
	ii) Document Classification	—	50	50		

4	Information Technology: Basics					
	i) Theory	50	—	50	100	120
	ii) Practice	—	50	50	—	—
5	Management of Libraries, InformationCentres / Institutions	—	—	100	100	120
6	Information Sources and Services (Th)	—	—	100	100	120
7	Information Sources and Services (Pr)	—	—	100	100	120
	i) Study of Information Sources	—	—	50	50	—
	ii) Compilation of Local Doc.Lists	—	—	50	50	—
8	Library Users	—	—	—	100	120
	i) Theory	50	—	50		
	ii) Practice	—	50	—		
	a) Library Field Survey	—	25	50		
	b) User Survey	—	25	100		
9	Fundamentals of Information Science	—	—	100	100	120
10	Information Analysis, Repackaging & Consolidation	—	—	—	100	120
	i) Theory	50	—			
	ii) Practice	—	50			
11	Information Retrieval	—	—	—	100	120
	i) Theory	50	—	50		
	ii) Practice	—	50	50		
12	Research Methods and Statistical Techniques	—	—	100	100	120
13	Information Technology Application (Th)	100	—	100	100	120
14	Information Technology Application (Pr)	—	100	100	100	120
15	Electives: Information Systems	—	—	—	100	—
	i) Theory	50	—	50		
	ii) Practice	—	50	50		
16	Dissertation/Project Work	80	20	100	100	120

Similarly for MLISc (Integrated / Semester Course) MLISc / Semester 2 Year programme (64 credits) Breakup of allotted study hours was provided at Page 49 in Tabular form which was as follows:

Paper No.	Paper Title:	T	A	S	P	H	C	F
1	Foundations of Library & Information Science	80	25	15	—	120	4	120
2	Knowledge Organization, Information Processing and Retrieval (Theory)	80	25	15	—	120	4	100
3	Knowledge Organization, Information Processing and Retrieval (Practice)	20	40	—	60	120	4	100
4	Information Technology (Basics)	40	20	—	60	120	4	100
5	Management of Libraries and Information Centres/ Institutions	80	25	15	—	120	4	100
6	Information Sources and Services (Theory)	80	25	15	—	120	4	100
7	Information Sources and Service (Practice)							
	i) Study of Information Sources	10	50					
	ii) Compilation of Local Doc. List	10	50					
8	Library Users	50	10	—	60	120	4	100
9	Fundamentals of Information Science	80	25	15	—	—	4	100
10	Information Analysis, Repackaging, Consolidation	50	10	—	60	120	4	100
11	Information Retrieval	50	10	—	60	120	4	100
12	Research Methods & Statistical Techniques	80	25	15	—	120	4	100
13	Information Technology: Applications (Theory)	80	25	15	—	120	4	100
14	Information Technology: Application (Practice)	20	20	—	80	120	4	100
15	Electives: Information Systems: i)Theory ii)Practice	50	50	10	10	120	4	100
16	Dissertation / Project Work	—	—	—	—	120	4	100

Note : T — Teaching; A — Assignment; S — Seminar; P — Practice; H — Hours; C — Credits and F — Full Marks.

The allotment of marks for Theory, Internal Assessment / Practice, Exam Marks, Total Marks and Teaching Hours appears to be more academic and idealistic rather than its practicability given the situation obtaining in the Departments of Library and Information Science in the Country. Likewise the allotment of credits and breakup of allotted study hours for MLISc 2-years programme (Integrated / Semester Course) was also an academic exercise and it was doubtful how many Departments of Library & Information Science in the Country can implement the credit system and allotted study hours.

Distance Education in LIS: Norms and Standards

The Committee took into consideration the emergence and fast growth of distance education in the country and offering Courses in LIS in the distance mode. The norms and standards for LIS programmes in the Country through distance mode developed by Distance Education Council (DEC) in 1996 were examined by the Curriculum Development Committee and accepted them with certain modifications as listed under:

1. For admission to BLISc Programme the following eligibility may be accepted in order of preference:
   a) Graduate with two years of working experience in a library.
   b) Graduate with Diploma / Certificate in Library Science.
   c) Professional graduates (Law, Pharmacy, Engineering).
   d) Graduates with 50% marks.
2. Increase in counselling / contact programme (study hours) both for theory as well as practice.

3. Introduction of compulsory Computer Practical for both BLISc and MLISc Students.
4. Curriculum designed by CDC / UGC should be followed by ICC's and O.U.
5. Provision of internship should be introduced for all BLISc students and should also expose to different libraries and their organizational pattern and services offered (visit to libraries).
6. Committee strongly recommends the adequate infrastructure in Headquarters and in every study centre, so that professional standards would be maintained properly. (Computer Hardware and Software, Classification Schedules, Cataloguing Codes and Reference Sources).
7. Orientation programmes should be organized by ICC's and Open Universities to make the Counsellors known about the latest developments in different Countries.

It was rather difficult to find out how many Open Universities / Distance Education / Correspondence Education Schools have been following the above norms and standards for imparting BLISc / MLISc Programmes.

Other Aspects of the Report

The Report appends four Annexures viz: I. Composition of Subject Panel on Library and Information Science, II. Conveners of BOS, III. Composition of Curriculum Development Committee Group I – III and IV: UGC D.O. Letter No.F.4-1/97 (Desk Panel), UGC D.O. Letter No.F.4-1/97 (Desk Panel) (Pages 55-67).

After the four Annexures we find in Part-II (Pages 75-147) Status Report on Library & Information Science

Education in India. This Part-II includes: 1. Introduction; 2. Status of LIS Education in India; 3. Academic Programmes; 4. Continuing Education Programmes; 5. Distance Education in LIS; 6. Summing up on Academic Programmes; 7. Infrastructure facilities, and 8. Conclusion. At the end, three appendices: 1. List of Library Science Departments / Colleges; 2. List of Library Science Course Programmes conducted by Universities; Colleges and Associations from whom the details are not received and 3. Library and Information Science Education through Distance Education were enclosed.

This Chapter (Part-II) was useful in a sense that it offers a bird's eye view of LIS Education in the Country in all its facets and strengths and weaknesses of Departments of LIS offering BLISc / MLISc / MLISc (2 year) and research Courses like M.Phil and Ph.D. programmes.

Utility of the Report

The Convener of UGC Panel on Library and Information Science Prof. C. R. Karisiddappa in his preface to the Report opined that "the Report is intended to be useful for Board of Studies of Departments of Library and Information Science in Indian Universities... The present Report is culmination of efforts and contributions made by a large number of Library and Information Science Teachers and practicing Librarians who deliberated intc different meetings organized and sponsored by UGC for this purpose. This massive participation of Library and Information Science experts from different parts of the Country in preparation of the Report, gives this Report the character and magnitude of *Saraswat Maha Yajna* which is expected to benefit all" (p.iii).

Adoption of Model Curriculum

Dr. Hari Gautam, the then Chairman, UGC in his 'Foreword' to the Report of CDC urged the concerned Universities "to adopt it in toto or to adopt it after making any change whatsoever which the University may consider right". He further stated that "the University Grants Commission requests the Hon'ble Registrars to confirm that this time bound exercise has been done and send a copy of the University's updated curriculum in each subject to UGC by July 1, 2002. It is a must. It has to be done timely, failing which, the UGC may be forced to take an appropriate unpleasant action against the concerned University".

In spite of this 'warning' it was rather difficult to find out how many LIS Departments in the Country had adopted the UGC Model Curriculum in LIS partially or fully to suit their local requirements.

It was more than a decade, that the "UGC Model Curriculum: Library and Information Science" was released for consideration and adoption by LIS Departments in the Country. The model curriculum has become somewhat outdated due to emergence of new concepts / areas especially in the field of Information and Communication technologies. There may be few LIS Departments in the Country which might have followed some of the recommendations made by the Prof. Karisiddappa Committee. The Board of Studies of LIS Departments in their annual meetings may be bringing some changes in their LIS Curriculum by including newly emerging concepts to meet their local requirements. So far no study has been made on the impact of 'model curriculum' on curricula being followed by LIS Departments / Schools in India. The UGC Model Curriculum had become a document of academic importance for study and research.

5.9. NATIONAL KNOWLEDGE COMMISSION, GOVERNMENT OF INDIA

Working Group (WG) on Libraries (2005)

The Government of India constituted the National Knowledge Commission[16] (NKC) in the year 2005 as a "High level Advisory Body to the Prime Minister of India with a mandate to guide policy and generate reforms". The Prime Minister in his inaugural address to the Commission on 2nd August 2005 stated that "the time has come to create a second wave of institution building and of excellence in the fields of education, research and capability building so that we are better prepared for the 21st Century.

The Commission as one of its first initiatives undertook to review the Library Services and to examine the present standards of Public, Private institutional and Specialized Libraries and other Information Centres. A Working Group (WG) on libraries consisting eminent Librarians and LIS Teachers was constituted "to initiate objective review of current services and standards and to recommend the changes India needs" with Smt. Kalpana Dasgupta as its Chair Person.

There were nine terms of reference of which reference sixth was to "Suggest means of raising standards and promoting excellence in Library and Information Science Education including re-orientation and training of working Professionals". To carry out its mandate the Working Group (WG) has setup four Committees viz;

1. Committee on Database Creation,
2. Committee on Private Collections,

3. Committee to set standards and modalities for collection development, and
4. Committee on Staffing Pattern and Staff Requirements of Libraries.

The WG has made a total of twenty nine recommendations covering areas such as: *LIS Policy, Finance, Library Management, Access and Networking, Private Collections, Digitization and Open Access, Staffing Pattern and Private Public Partnership.* But there was no specific recommendation on the state of LIS Education in the Country.

The WG has made a total twenty nine recommendations covering various facets such as: *1. LIS Policy, 2. Finance, 3. Library Management, 4. Private Collections, 5. Digitization and Open Access, 6. Staffing Pattern and 7. Public Private Partnership.* Under LIS Policy at Recommendation-V, the Committee recommended that "the LIS Education and Training (including in-service) should be revised and revamped. The Mission on Libraries must assess as soon as possible the manpower requirements of the Country in the area of LIS management and take necessary steps to meet the Country's requirement through LIS education and training". (P.3).

Under Appendix 10: Staffing Pattern and Staff Requirement of Libraries (P.28) at Recommendation-V: Staffing Pattern of LIS Departments (P.32) the WG recommended as follows:

1. A System should be set up to foster close cooperation between the teaching / research faculty and practicing librarians at all academic and research institutions, by measures such as:
   I. Mobility of Staff (in terms of recruitment and in terms of teaching) should be made possible.

II. Practicing librarians and experts should be associated with the teaching faculty for offering specialized courses.

III. Similarly, teachers could be associated with libraries as consultants, for carrying out projects, and for carrying out continuing education programmes to practicing librarians, etc.

2. The minimum staffing pattern for the BLISc Course should be as follows:

I.	Professor	1
II.	Reader	1
III.	Lecturers	2

3. The minimum staffing pattern for MLISc Course should beas follows:

I.	Professor	1
II.	Reader	2
III.	Lecturers	4

4. There should be a 1: 10 student-teacher ratio.

5. It was felt that the Department should have not more than 50 students in one class for BLISc Course and 20 students for MLISc Course and Ph.D. students according to University norms.

6. All Departments of LIS should setup Computer Laboratories and well equipped departmental libraries with appropriate teaching tools.

7. Appropriate physical facilities such as class rooms, must be made available to each LIS Department.

8. E-learning materials for upgrading the skills of the existing staff should be provided.

9. Teachers, who will teach in areas such as ICT

applications in Libraries and other modern methods, should have specialized in these areas. A system should be set up to allow stringent review of the performance of teachers. A suitable system of rewards, including promotion, should be instituted.

Besides Recommendation-V, which deals with LIS education and training, and Recommendation-VI : Staffing Pattern of LIS Departments (in Appendix 10), the WG has not recommended any specific curriculum for LIS Schools in India for conducting BLISc / MLISc Courses. As far LIS education in the country is concerned, the WG has not made any specific recommendation(s) with regards syllabi, working hours, allocation of marks for each paper, practical component in BLISc / MLISc Courses being conducted in India. In other words the WG has made a passing reference to LIS education in the Country.

Indian Institute of Library and Information Science (ILIS)

The WG under Recommendation-VI recommended for setting up "a separate and well equipped Institution for Advanced Training and Research in Library and Information Science and Service". The details for this Institution were spelled out in Appendix-3 (P.12).

In Appendix-3, the proposed Institution was named as "Indian Institute of Library and Information Science (ILIS)" with the following two major functions:

a) To offer training programmes in relevant areas and to conduct continuing education programmes (including training of trainers) for the Library and Information Professionals.

b) To identify, sponsor and conduct R & D programmes in the field of Library and Information Science, including newly emerging research areas. Among the areas needing immediate R & D, the following were identified by the Working Group (WG).

- User needs for different groups.
- Reading habits.
- Organization of Community Information and Development of Appropriate Standards.
- Standardization of Indian names.
- Vocabulary Control over Indian Subjects developed in terms of multilingual thesauri and subject heading lists.
- Development of Open Source Software.
- Development of Digital Libraries, both in English and Indian Languages.
- Technical Standards for Indian Scripts, Optical Character Recognition (OCR) for Indian Scripts, and search engines which can implement stemming algorithms for Indian languages.
- Cross Language Information Retrieval with an emphasis on information in Indian Languages". (Pp.12-13).

A Standing Committee was appointed to implement the recommendations of the WG on Libraries appointed by the National Knowledge Commission. Not much is known about the implementation of the recommendations of the WG by the Standing Committee. The initial euphoria that something good will be done to the development of libraries in the Country has slowly dissipated. Now there is less talk among the library professionals, librarians and LIS teachers about the recommendations of WG on Libraries.

National Mission on Libraries

As per the recommendations of National Knowledge Commission (NKC) and its Working Group (WG) on Libraries, at last the Ministry of Culture, Government of India notified the establishment "National Mission on Libraries on 4th May 2012[17], with eleven terms of reference. The sixth term of reference deals with reviewing and assessing current Status of library and Information Science education and service, training facilities and working with agencies such as the UGC and Universities to address the identified issues. A high level Committee was constituted under the Chairmanship of Prof. Deepak Pental, former Vice-Chancellor of University of Delhi along with nine other members for a period of three years. The Secretary, Ministry of Culture was the Member Secretary of the said Committee. One has to wait and see the role to be played by the mission for the cause of L IS education in the Country.

It is pertinent to quote the opinion of IASLIC in not setting up Indian Institute of Library and Information Science (IILIS). It states that "it was extremely heartening to us (IASLIC) with the hope that this NML would give due importance in implementing all ten major recommendations including setting up the Indian Institute of Library and Information Science (IILIS) of national importance which, as a nodal body would give a vital direction to LIS education, research and practice for both high speed generation and use of knowledge needed for bringing a structural change in Indian economy. IASLIC demands that the IILIS is absolutely the need of the hour for the LIS profession of Library and Information Science to fulfill its role as a "Corner stone of the knowledge society..... But unfortunately NML has not taken any positive step to this effect. At least we could not find any such prominent effort on the part of NML"[18].

REFERENCES

1. *University and College Libraries.* New Delhi, UGC, 1965. P.228.
2. *Library Science in Indian Universities.* New Delhi, UGC, 1965. P.86.
3. *Report of Advisory Committee for Libraries.* New Delhi, Ministry of Education, Government of India, 1961. P.102.
4. Ibid, p.94.
5. *Library Science in Indian Universities.* Opcit.P.86.
6. *Report of the Committee appointed by Government of Andhra Pradesh* in February 1976 to Review the Working of Andhra Pradesh Public Libraries Act, 1960. Hyderabad, Dept. of Public Libraries, Got. Of A.P., 19789. P.185.
7. Letter dated November 22, 1991 from the Secretary, UGC addressed to Prof. A. A. N. Raju who was nominated as Member of Panel in Library and Information Science from November 1991 for a period of two year term.
8. Recommendations of the Panel on Library and Information Science. New Delhi; UGC, 1982 (Mimeographed).
9. Ibid. P.3.
10. Raju, A. A. N. The Chequered History of Library and Information Science Curriculum. *University News* V37, N34, August 23, 1991. Pp.6-10.
11. *Report of the Curriculum Development Committee on Library and Information Science.* New Delhi, UGC, 1992.P157.
12. Raju, A.A.N. The Chequered History of Library and Information Science Curriculum. Opcit. Pp.6-10.
13. Large, J.A. *A Modular Curriculum for Information Studies.* Paris, UNESCO, 1987.
14. *UGC Model Curriculum: Library and Information Science,* New Delhi, UGC, 2001. P.147.
15. Ibid.

16. Libraries: Gateways to Knowledge: A Roadmap for Revitalization. New Delhi, National Knowledge Commission, 2007.

17. Ministry of Culture, Govt. of India. National Mission on Libraries. Notification dated 4th May, 2012. New Delhi, Ministry of Culture, Govt. of India, 2012.

18. *IASLIC News Letter*, November 2013. P.2.

6

Professional Associations Supporting The Cause of LIS Education

Professional Associations such as Indian Library Association (ILA), Delhi, Indian Association of Special Libraries and Information Centres (IASLIC), Kolkata and Indian Association of Teachers of Library and Information Science (IATLIS) have contributed in their own way for the growth and development of LIS education in the Country by organizing National, State and Regional level Conferences / Seminars for the cause of Library and Information Science Education in the Country. Especially ILA and IASLIC through their professional journals such as *ILA Bulletin* (now Journal of ILA) and *IASLIC Bulletin* provide ample space to cover various facets of LIS education in the Country. Many research articles, seminar / conference reports, recommendations and resolutions are being published in the pages of these journals. Especially the *Newsletters* brought out by ILA, IASLIC and IATLIS cover the events happened already and forthcoming events concerning LIS education and thus brining to the notice of LIS teaching fraternity current developments on various facets of LIS education in the Country.

6.1. INDIAN ASSOCIATION OF TEACHERS OF LIBRARY AND INFORMATION SCIENCE (IATLIS)

This Professional Association exclusively formed to take care of LIS teachers interests in the country was established in the year 1969. A meeting of teachers of LIS attending Annual Sarada Ranganathan Endowment Lecture held at DRTC, Bangalore was convened on December 19, 1969 by Prof. P. N. Kaula. Prof. D. B. Krishna Rao one of the participants asked Prof. Kaula to state the purpose of the meeting. Prof. Kaula in his opening remarks stressed the need for having 'Association of LIS teachers'. Dr. Krishna Rao opined that Indian Association of Teachers of Library and Information Science (IATLIS) be formed with an ad-hoc Committee for the purpose. Thus a Committee was formed with Prof. Krishna Rao as its Chairman and Prof. Kaula as its Secretary. This was the genesis of a national professional body of LIS teachers (IATLIS) to further the cause of LIS education in the Country[1]. This professional body though not dynamic as was expected by its members, helped in its own way, through the four and half decades of its existence, the growth, development and spread of LIS education in the country through its annual conferences / seminars / newsletters and other publications covering various facets of LIS education.

IATLIS: National Seminars / Conferences

This professional body right from 1970, an year after its establishment organized annual national conferences / seminars covering various facets of LIS education. Right from 1970 till 2011 the Association organized 28 National Conferences / Seminars. The following Table provides details of these Conferences / Seminars.

Sl. No.	Dates	Host	Theme
1	19-21 Dec.1970	DRTC, Bangalore	First Annual Seminar *"Teaching Methods in Library Science".*
2	09-11 March,1973	DLISc, Karnatak University Dharwad	Second IATLIS National Seminar *"Graduate Library Education Programme: BLISc".*
3	13-18 March,1981	DLISc, Banaras Hindu University, Varanasi	*"Relevance of LIS Education to the changing needs of the Country".*
4	09-10 Nov. 1986	DLISc, University of Lucknow, Lucknow	*"Use of Audio-Visual Aids in LIS Teaching".*
5	21-23Nov. 1988	DLISc, Gulbarga University, Gulbarga	*"Education for Academic Librarianship".*
6	14-16Dec. 1989	DLISc, Saurashthra University, Rajkot	*"Reconstructing LIS Curriculum".*
7	31 Jan. to 2 Feb. 1991	DLISc, Bangalore University,Bangalore	?
8	?	?	?
9	26-28 August 1991	DLISc, Andhra University, Visakhapatnam	*"Standards for LIS Education".*
10	03-05 Nov.1992	DLISc, University of Poona,Pune	*"Learning Material in LIS in India".*
11	03-06 June, 1994	SMIT, Ankuspur (Orissa)	*"Research in LIS in India".*
12	21-22 April 1995	DLISc, Kerala University, Trivandrum	*"Infrastructure Facilities for LIS Schools".*
13	26-27 January 1996	DLISc, Babasaheb Ambedkar University, Aurangabad	*"Themes for Continuing Education of Library Professionals in India".*
14	25-27Nov. 1996	DLISc, Osmania University, Hyderabad	*"Information Technology and its Impact on LIS Education and Management".*
15	27-29Nov. 1997	DLISc, University of Mysore, Mysore	*"Fifty Years of LIS Education in India".*
16	08-10January 1998	DLISc, Gulbarga	*"Application of IT in India:*

		University, Gulbarga	*Status, Strategies, Opportunities and Problems".*
17	1st Week of Feb. 2001	DLISc, University of Kerala, Trivandrum	*"Library and Information Science Education in the Internet Era".*
18	12-14 October, 2001	DLISc, Andhra University, Visakhapatnam	*"Changing Dimensions of LIS Education".*
19	01-03Dec. 2002	DLISc, Utkal University, Bhubaneshwar	*"Manpower Development for Information Management in Competitive Environment".*
20	21-23 Nov. 2003	DLISc, University of Madras, Chennai	*"Globalization of LIS Education".*
21	18-20Nov. 2004	DLISc, Nagpur University, Nagpur	*"Partnership of LIS Teachers and Librarians in Professional Development".*
22	24-26Nov. 2005	Trichy	*"Quality Education in Library and Information Science".*
23	23-25Nov. 2006	DLISc, Panjabi University, Patiala	*"Building Curriculum with a Difference: A Vision for LIS Education in the 21st Century".*
24	19-21 Nov. 2007	DLISc, Karnatak University, Dharwad	*"Equity of LIS Education in IT based Pedagogical Environment of the Knowledge Society".*
25	2008	DLISc, Panjab University, Chandigarh	*"Changing Facet of LIS Education: Learning Styles and Teaching Methodologies".*
26	2009	DLISc, Panjabi University, Patiala	*"Envisioning Employable LIS Courses in Developing Countries for the emerging Knowledge Society".*
27	2010	DLISc, University of Poona,Pune	*"Emerging and Lingering Issues in LIS Education, Research and Training".*
28	26-28Nov. 2011	DLISc, Gujarat University, Ahmedabad	*"LIS Education, Research and Training: Vision 2020".*

20	20-22March, 2013	DRTC, Bangalore (Golden Jubilee National Conference on LIS Education)	*"LIS Education and Research: Contemplating Persistent and Debatable Issues".*

Recommendations of some of the IATLIS National Conferences

Recommendations of 14th IATLIS / AGLIS National Seminar held at Osmania University, Hyderabad during 25-27 November 1996:

1. The Seminar recognized the Impact of IT on the education sector in general and LIS education in particular. It is, therefore, recommended that the IT and its by-products such as Internet, CD-ROM and E-mail should be increasingly and effectively used in LIS Education.
2. The Seminar noted with satisfaction the inclusion of IT in the syllabi of LIS programmes in the library schools in India. The IT papers at present confined only to theoretical aspects. The Seminar realized the need for practical experience to the outgoing students of the library schools and strongly recommended that there should be one practical paper in IT to provide hands on experience to the students.
3. It is further recommended that the LIS students may have internship in libraries which have IT environment for gaining practical experience and confidence.
4. The Seminar unanimously recommended that the UGC, DST, Planning Commission and the University authorities may be approached for financial support during the ninth plan period for establishing Computer Laboratories and the necessary infrastructure in the Library Schools.

5. The multimedia technology has vast potentiality and utility for teaching LIS subjects. Hence, the multimedia products should be acquired by the library schools.
6. The Seminar suggested that appropriate agencies in the country be requested to prepare the multimedia products keeping in view the introduction of IT into the course curriculum. Further, the multimedia products should be cost effective and easily available.
7. It is unanimously felt that an IT environment may be created in all types of LICs in the Country. Further, the Seminar recommended that the LICs should adopt IT in their management and offer value added services to the community.
8. It is recommended that the academic and special libraries should create necessary facilities to have access to data and information through internet and other local, regional, national and international databases and networks.
9. The Seminar recognized the need, relevance and utility of the continuing education programmes in IT for the LIS teachers, librarians and information specialists. It is therefore recommended that short-term and long-term programmes such as Seminars, Symposia and Workshops may be organized at regular intervals by agencies like DST, NIC, INSDOC, INFLIBNET, Library Schools and Library Associations.
10. LICs in the Country should explore avenues of revenue generation, resource mobilization and resource sharing with the help of IT.

Source: IATLIS Communication, V16, N4, October-December, 1996.Pp 1-2.

Recommendations of 15th IATLIS National Seminar held at University of Mysore, Mysore from 27-29 November, 1997.

1. Course Duration : There are two streams of LIS education in India, that is BLISc and MLISc degree programmes of one year duration each and that of two year integrated Master's degree programme. In view of the fact that a large number of Universities are yet to implement the latter and that UGC-CDC has also made a suggestion in this regard of proposing the two streams, it is resolved that the stream of Courses to be offered to be left to the choice of individual Universities. It is further resolved that Master's degree awarded through the two year programme and one year programme should be considered as equivalent.

2. Products of LIS Literature in Regional Media : In view of ongoing trend among students to study and write their examinations in regional languages and to provide an opportunity for those students who are unable to assimilate the subject in English language, it is resolved to encourage teachers and library professionals to write text books in regional language through team work and through translation. It is also recommended to compile multi-lingual dictionaries and glossaries in LIS to support this work.

Further, it is also resolved to approach various bodies such as Academies, Bureaus, Directorates and UGC for technical and financial assistance in this regard.

3. Course Content : The LIS Course Content is influenced by within and outside purview and there is marked dependability to study the traditional (core) areas and new emerging areas finding integration in LIS Curriculum. It is resolved to restructure LIS

Curriculum in a balanced manner by integrating core and peripheral areas.

4. Infrastructure Facilities : It is observed that majority of LIS Schools are lacking adequate infrastructural facilities to teach / train LIS students in IT. Hence, it is recommended that the UGC should provide special financial assistance to develop adequate, need based IT infrastructure facilities in L IS Schools.

5. Review of LIS Programmes : A Comprehensive Review Committee on LIS was appointed in 1960s and its report was accepted in 1965. Since then no such comprehensive review of LIS programmes has been taken up or carried out. Hence it is recommended to appoint a UGC Review Committee to go through the entire scheme of educational programmes in LIS and to suggest suitable measures to improve LIS education to be capable to meet current and future challenges of the profession.

6. Distance Education : It is recommended that the LIS programmes offered through distance education should be improved qualitatively and also be evaluated periodically by a competent authority.

7. Regulatory Mechanism : The LIS education in India has crossed its Platinum Jubilee and a body to regulate, evaluate and suggest education and research programmes in LIS is a long felt need. Hence, it is resolved to recommend the establishment of a "National Council for LIS Education and Research".

8. Accreditation : Keeping in view the recommendations made at various national forums in the past to formulate necessary standards and norms to evaluate and improve the LIS education programme, it is recommended that an accreditation mechanism be created on the lines of AICTE, MCI, BCI, etc.

This mechanism, besides bringing quality improvement in LIS education, will also help in assisting those schools which require support financially and otherwise to raise to the standard levels.

9. LIS Research : Since 1950s LIS research has been initiated and an upward trend is noticed from mid 1970s. To promote this healthy trend and also to guide future research programmes, it is recommended that a research database be prepared as an inventory of research carried out in LIS.

Source: *IATLIS Communication V17, N4 – V18, N1 October 1997 – March 1998. Pp.3-4.*

Resolutions of 18th IATLIS National Seminar held at the Dept. of Library and Information Science, Andhra University, Visakhapatnam during October 12-14, 2001:

1. "To design and develop viable and practical oriented curriculum with specialization in LIS education.
2. The LIS teachers shall be constantly exposed to the modern skills and techniques of information technology, imparting effective education and training.
3. To provide adequate facilities to build up competency in designing and developing teaching methods, skills and techniques by the concerned agencies such as UGC, NCERT, INFLIBNET, Distance Education Councils and Professional Organizations.
4. To create healthy and dynamic LIS professionals to face future challenges, appraise constantly with the emerging trends and vital developments in the LIS field".

Source: *ALSD Communication, Nos.101 and 102, July – December, 2001. P.8*

Resolutions of the 19th IATLIS National Seminar held at the Dept. of Library and Information Science, Utkal University, Bhubaneshwar from 1-3, December, 2002:

1. "To cope up the pass-outs of the existing library schools in the country to the competitive technological environment, there should be a balance between technologies oriented approach and the user oriented approach in the curricula of LIS Schools.
2. LIS Departments need to procure required infrastructure to train the students in the new technological environment. The teachers of the departments should frequently involve the practicenors in designing courses, curricula and identification of research priorities.
3. In order to generate suitable manpower to face and tackle the dynamic environment, the library professionals and the professional associations like IATLIS should work out the basic levels of training, the training strategies, and policies to enable the library schools to implement with uniformity.
4. To make the existing curricula suitable to generate specialized manpower in the changing environment, efforts should be made to design two types of courses i.e. 1) general courses for traditional librarianship with larger duration and 2) specialized courses for special interest groups with shorter duration. Library Organizations, institutions and associations should cooperate to establish, organize and implement the shorter courses".

Source: IATLIS Communication V22, N4 - V23, N1 December 2002– March 2003. P.4.

Recommendations and Resolutions of the 20th IATLIS National Conference held at University of Madras, Chennai during 21-23 November, 2003:

1. "In the context of Globalization and ICT developments on the one hand and the existing (limited) resources such as infrastructure, faculty, information resources, etc. in Indian LIS Schools, it is recommended the LIS Schools adopt strategies for:
   a) Formation of consortia to enable to share expertise and resources which will have greater impact in offering quality programmes;
   b) Design of modular curricula that would be useful and acceptable nationally and globally, permitting the students to complete various modules among the LIS schools at National and International levels.
   c) Development of appropriate course materials – traditional and electronic – useful for formal, distance education and continuing education programmes.
   d) Accreditation by recognized national and international agencies.
   e) Establishment of linkages and relationships with professionals of other countries through professional associations.
   f) Teacher training with emphasis on application of innovative teaching methods, techniques and materials as well as in the application of information technology.
   g) Promoting industry – institute relationship to provide employment for students.

h) Marketing of their LIS education programmes to other nations / countries.

2. Realizing the various revolutionary and innovative developments such as information revolution, ICT revolution, globalization and privatization on the one hand and recognition of an urgent need for imparting quality education and training by the Indian LIS Schools:

   It is recommended that LIS schools and Library Associations should:

   a) Adapt and adopt new instructional technological instruments in LIS teaching and developing models for Computer Based Teaching (CBT)

   b) Use Internet and other communication technologies to enable share resources and communicate and hereby provide education and training through its varied potential and particularly by e-learning / network learning.

   c) Organize and conduct refresher courses, teacher training programmes and workshops highlighting the facets of computer based teaching and learning as well as use of ICT and now particularly Internet both as a source and tool in globalization of LIS education, etc.

3. Realizing that there are many inadequacies in existing LIS education programmes due to prevailing diversity in – information environments, student population, faculty, course structures, resources available etc – and recognizing that globalization demands for development of LIS education programmes that are locally and internationally acceptable.

It is recommended that LIS Schools:

a) Redesign their curricula to suit with local and global requirements by including relevant modules with special emphasis on IT applications.

b) Empowering their faculty through – training programmes, motivational methods, provision of funds for paper based and electronic resources as well as for training / teaching materials; promotion of collaboration within and outside the departments in teaching, research, etc.

4. Realizing and recognizing that the self-life of skills acquired by the Faculty and other information professionals is decreasing continuously and coupled with the phenomenon of the information overload, info stress and changing contours of the market for LIS professionals.

It is recommended that:

Library Associations like IATLIS, IASLIC, ILA, SISs, etc. and Government & Non-Governmental organizations like UGC, RRRLF should sponsor and fund different types of LIS education programmes – formal, distance education / on-line education and continuing education programmes for different types of professionals with a view:

a) To design and develop need based programmes with appropriate modular curricula keeping the developments taking place the world over.

b) To prepare course materials – traditional and electronic for the different programmes.

c) To organize and conduct training

programmes for teachers; workshops, refresher courses, seminars, user-education programmes and similar programmes for faculty development and empowerment highlighting both content and pedagogical techniques.

d) To conduct research investigations in LIS to strengthen the research base and similar programmes in pursuit of academic excellence.

5. Realizing that the present LIS education is in a state of disarray due to diversity in approaches and recognizing the need to maintain high academic standards in LIS education programmes to facilitate globalization.

It is recommended that:

A professional organization / agency at a national level be established so that it can undertake the work of accreditation of the Courses and Departments / Institutions concerned, on lines similar to the Medical Council of India and Bar Council of India.

6. Recognizing that the information resources and services in information handling institutions like libraries are underutilized.

It is recommended that:

LIS Schools design elementary curricula dealing with effective utilization of information sources and services to facilitate introduction of information literacy programmes in schools and colleges.

7. In view of the differential needs of information professionals and the fact that no one LIS School can achieve excellence in all fields of LIS.

It is recommended that:

Agencies like UGC, RRRLF, etc., should sponsor and fund for the development of schools of excellence in specialized areas of LIS at the different Department of LIS in different academic institutions in the country.

Source: IATLIS Communications, V23, N4, Dec.2003 and V24, N1, 2, 3, January-September 2004. Pp.6-7.

Resolutions of the 21st IATLIS National Seminar held at DLISc, Nagpur University, Nagpur during 18-20 November, 2004.

1. Taking note of the financial burden on the students of LIS schools, it is resolved to request the UGC to provide some stipend / remuneration to the students for the period of internship.
2. Realizing the need for cooperation and collaboration between the libraries and LIS teaching departments for professional development, the conference recommends the following ways and means for effective partnership.
   I. The Departments have to work in coherence with working librarians and library professionals since the discipline requires more interaction within the profession.
   II. Course management teams can be devised for each course / paper after defining the theoretical and practical components. Team-teaching by sharing the experience and infrastructure will certainly bridge the existing gap.
   III. Librarians and experienced professionals support be sought for the collaborative approach in imparting practical skills.

IV. All the librarians have a professional obligation to contribute to the education and training of LIS students.

V. The librarians have to maintain a high standard of professional and personal traits so that the students acquire proper professional attitudes, skills and knowledge.

3. In view of the specialized skills to be acquired by the professionals in the present information age, the conference has identified the following areas for emphasis in LIS teaching:

   I. Automation and Network aspects.

   II. Spoken English training / teaching programmes to upgrade the language skills of incoming professionals.

Source: IATLIS Communications, V24, N4. October-December, 2004 and V25, N1, January – March 2005. P.4.

Recommendations and Resolutions of 22nd IATLIS National Conference held at Trichy from 24 - 26 November, 2005:

1. "In view of the growing impact of globalization the quality issue with reference to LIS education be taken seriously to produce the quality manpower of high competence.

   It is recommended that:

   a) The NAC should take immediate measures to develop norms for accreditation of LIS programmes to ensure the quality education and training.

   b) It is also recommended that the UGC, AICTE, NAAC and DEC have to appoint an expert committee to develop a set of quality norms

/ standards and ensure their implementation uniformly in all LIS Departments in India.

2. Realizing the greater impact of IT on Library and Information Services and to prepare the competent manpower.

   It is recommended that:

   The UGC should take appropriate steps to regularly revise LIS Curriculum at different levels.

3. Considering the prevalence of traditional teaching techniques and methods in majority of the LIS schools and impact of ever-growing educational technology on teaching and research.

   It is recommended that:

   UGC may take necessary steps to initiate and to provide online learning facilities by exploring the possibility of using newly launched EDUSAT both for formal and distance students.

4. It is revolved that every LIS School must incorporate hands on experience in the LIS programmes up to 30% of the curriculum, both for formal and distance students.

5. Looking at the complexity of skills required to handle information, it is resolved that the internship programmes should be made compulsory to provide confidence and competence to the LIS products.

   It is recommended that:

   The appropriate authorities like UGC, DEC, etc, need to formulate the suitable norms and standards to maintain the quality LIS education for (Distance mode students) in the Country".

Source: IATLIS Communications. V26, N.122. June to July 2006. P.2.

Recommendations of 23rd IATLIS National Conference held at Panjabi University, Patiala during 23-25 November, 2006:

1. "The curriculum for the LIS programmes in the Country should become a collective effort hence there is need that the LIS Professional Community to actively participate towards the formulation of National Curriculum Policy.
2. The LIS being practice oriented profession internship has been an integral part of teaching programme. The LIS Departments are following different modes of internship programmes, hence there is need for uniform policy for internship in terms of duration and the mode of the implementation.
3. The learning of learners is an important component; hence there is need for more awareness needed for the continued education programmes for teachers of LIS.
4. For the Development of teaching programmmes and closer interaction among educators of LIS there is need for faculty and students exchange should be encouraged and appropriate mechanism should be worked out in this regard.
5. The accreditation of LIS Departments is a often discussed in various forums and there is need for instituting an agency for accreditation of Department and there is also need for formulation of norms and need for accreditation of individual departments.
6. There is over growth of distance education programmes in LIS, it is also need of the hour due to need for facilitating the unprivileged, however it is essential that there is need for

quality control of LIS education offered through distance mode and to check undesirable growth of such programmes.

7. For the active involvement of the LIS students in societal programmes, the library science graduates must be trained for community information services for the rural areas both for employment and for the social development of rural communities.
8. In the days of outsourcing and self employment trends emerging, it is desirable that the Departments of LIS should train the students to be fit for employment related areas such as IT Services, self-entrepreneurships, e-publishing, etc.
9. The school library is neglected sector and there is need for focusing school library as they can play a very vital role in popularizing library culture among children and in inculcating pursuits among the young minds.
10. Due to rapid changes and paradigm shift in the environment of LIS and the related fringe areas, it is necessary to look for the revolutionary changes in the syllabus after every three years to keep in tune with the social and market trends.
11. During 1960s a beginning was made for the South-Asian dialogue on economic front and in information front. Much collaborative efforts were not initiated in the information sector then, but due to influence of the IT on LIS it is now easy and imperative and developing countries must come together to interaction issues of LIS education. There must be more interact on and exchange of ideas among the SAARC Countries

LIS educators and Librarians and then the collaborating among South Asian Countries.

12. The UGC model curriculum 2001 is almost five years old now and as it proposed in the recommendation-10. It is time for revise this curriculum at the national level and the UGC to consider this proposal very urgently. The resulting curriculum should be made mandatory for implementation by all the LIS Departments in the Country".

Source: IATLIS Communications, V28, N1 & 2. December, 2006.to May 2007, Pp.2-3.

6.2. INDIAN ASSOCIATION OF SPECIAL LIBRARIES AND INFORMATION CENTRES (IASLIC), KOLKATA

The establishment of Indian Association of Special Libraries and Information Centres, popularly known in professional circles as IASLIC on 3rd September 1955 at Calcutta was a landmark in the history of special librarianship in India. The stalwarts of the profession mainly based at Calcutta Sarvasri J. Saha, A. K. Mukharjee, G. B. Ghosh and other professionals took initiative in its establishment and nurtured at its formative periods to take strong roots for its sustained growth and development. Since its establishment the association carrying out its multifarious activities through organizing national seminars / conferences, workshops, symposia every year meticulously at local / regional / national and international levels, publication of professional journal ***IASLIC Bulletin***, and ***IASLIC Newsletter***, and bringing out monographs for the benefit of the professionals. During the six decades of its existence, IASLIC has grown from strength to strength and reached appreciable professional heights and carved out a niche in the domain of Special Librarianship in the country.

The Association in its own way contributed to the spread of LIS education in the country by organizing a couple of national conferences / seminars on LIS education and related topics, publishing articles on LIS education and research in its official organ *IASLIC Bulletin* and communicating news on LIS education through its *IASLIC Newsletter.*

So far IASLIC has organized 29 All India Conferences and equal number All India Seminars until 2013. For the first time, IASLIC in the year 1957 had organized a national conference on LIS Education titled "*Training for Special Librarianship in India*" at Calcutta[2]. Again in the year 1962 a national seminar on *"Education for Librarianship in India"* was organized at Panjab University, Chandigarh. For the third time IASLIC has organized another national conference on the topic *"Education for Special Library and Information Work"* in the year 1987 at Sri Venkateshwara University Tirupati.

Again IASLIC at its 24th National Seminar held during 18-21 December 2010 at Deen Dayal Upadhaya Gorakpur University, two themes viz. *1. Reading habits in changing scenario* and *2. LIS Education: Emerging Paradigm changes and Vision* were discussed and suitable recommendations were made. The recommendations pertaining to LIS Education were follows:

1. "In order to pursue excellence in LIS Education and weed out low and substandard courses, branding and accreditation similar to international standards such as ISO 9001 may be considered. The Seminar recommends creation

of an accreditation body for LIS courses on the line of NCTE and AICTE.

2. In view of globalization and increasing competition in the job market, concerted collaborative efforts must be made to make LIS teaching and learning programmes consistent with the emerging job market demands. Hence it is recommended to the UGC, AICTE, DEC and other concerned bodies to form an Expert Committee to work out an action plan to enhance LIS Education in our Country.
3. It is felt that LIS teachers should shift from traditional teaching methods to new methods especially ICT-based innovative teaching. It would help bringing confidence in the teachers. The NKC may be approached in this respect.
4. It is proposed to review the UGC Model Curriculum for LIS (2001) in view of later developments in the job market, emergence of new technologies and in respect of duration of courses, course content and structure.
5. In view of substantial difference between schools in terms of infrastructure, resources, duration of courses and faculty, it is recommended the UGC should take up the issue to bring the lagging LIS Schools to minimum standards. Provision should be made for exchange of teachers as well as virtual class rooms".

Source: IASLIC Newsletter, January 2011. P.2.

IASLIC at its 23rd National Seminar on the theme *"Library Profession in Search of a New Paradigm"* held at Bose Institute, Kolkata from 10-13, December, 2008, adapted the following resolution No.4. "The Seminar recognizes that in order to meet the changing requirements in services from different types of libraries and information centres in the Country, there is an urgent need for giving fresh look to Library and Information Science (LIS) programmes in the country. The Seminar urges upon the Universities / UGC and the Departments of Library and Information Science in the country to take early steps in this direction so that their students found to be more suitable to meet the challenging paradigms of the Library and Information Centres in the country"[3].

The Special Interest Groups 02 (SIG) at its meeting on 10th December 2008 under the theme *"Library and Information Science (LIS) Education"* adopted the following resolutions.

i. "The curriculum of LIS Schools should facilitate to train such individuals who could suit to the needs and market requirements in the present scenario of paradigm shift of the library and Information Services.

ii. Efforts should be made by all the Professional Associations to facilitate the enactment of National Policy for LIS Education. The proposed National Institute for LIS Education, recommended by the National Knowledge Commission is a positive step and the National Institute must be created without further delay.

iii. In order to provide suitable training to students, LIS Schools must introduce compulsory internship programme for a period of two months immediately after the examinations. Since LIS is a professional Course.

iv. Keeping in view the market demands, LIS schools should introduce by creating models for LIS Education such as (a) Corporate Librarianship; (b) Media Librarianship, etc"[4].

6.3. INDIAN LIBRARY ASSOCIATION (ILA), NEW DELHI

Dr. M. O. Thomas, the then Librarian, Andhra University contributed an article in January 1933 issue of *Modern Librarian* entitled *"An ideal Library Association"* in which he made out a case for an Indian Library Association. This article inspired library enthusiasts and in the April issue of Modern *Librarian*, printed an announcement about the holding of First All India Library Conference at Calcutta in September, 1933. The announcement carried the signatures of eminent librarians of the time which included among others Newton Mohan Dutt, J. A. Chapman, K. M. Asadullah, S. R. Ranganathan, R. V. Sabnis and S. Bashiruddin.

The Conference met in Asiatic Society Hall, Calcutta on 12th September 1933. On 13th September the draft constitution of Indian Library Association was adopted and thus Indian Library Association (ILA) came into being with the following objectives:

a) The furtherance of the Library Movement in India;

b) The promotion of training the librarians; and

c) The improvement of status of Librarians.

During the past eight decades of its existence, the Association organized National level Library Conferences at different places in the country. So far it has organized 59 National Conferences until the end of 2013 covering broad areas such as: *Library Classification and Cataloguing, Documentation, Reference Service, Stock Verification, Bibliographic Control, Library Education, Role of Libraries in National Development* and emerging areas such as: *Library and Information Services in the Electronic Information Era, A Quality Assurance in Libraries, IT Applications and*

Library Management, Users' need and Library Services in the internet era[5].

ILA has organized the first National Conference on LIS Education at its XI All India Conference during 7-11 April 1956 at Calcutta. The second National Conference on Library Research Programmes was held on 25th National Conference during 14-18 May 1979 at Trivandrum. The third National Conference on LIS Education was held at its 30th National Conference during 28-31 January 1984 at Jaipur. Besides these three National level Conferences on LIS Education, ILA through its official organ ***ILA Bulletin*** and now *Journal of Indian Library Association*, publishing articles on various facets of LIS education in the country. In addition *ILA Newsletter* also provides information on forthcoming Conferences / Seminars on various aspects of LIS including LIS Education.

REFERENCES

1. Kumar, PSG, Comp. Indian Library chronology. New Delhi, Metropolitan Book Co., 1977. P.384.
2. Chandra, Jaydeep and Saha, Ramakrishna. Bibliometric Analysis of IASLIC Conferences and Seminars: 1956-2004. *In* IASLIC: Challenges and Prospects. *Ed.* by Arjun Dasgupta and J. N. Satapathi. Kolkata, IASLIC, 2007. Pp.68-74.
3. Report of the 23rd National Seminar of IASLIC; Library Profession I Search of a New Paradigm. 10-13, December 2008. Bose Institute, Kolkata. Kolkata, IASLIC, 2008.P.47.
4. Ibid., Pp.15-16.
5. Shokeen, N. S. Steady Growth of ILA Conferences. In 53rd All India Library Conference of ILA *Souvenir*, DLISc, Osmania University, 2007. Pp.34-40.

7

LIS Research in India

7.1. INTRODUCTION

Libraries and Information Centers (LICs) play a vital role in the socio-economic development of a nation. The accelerated growth in Research and Developmental activities in Sciences and Technology and also in the fields of Social Sciences and Humanities contributed to a phenomenal growth in the Universe of subjects resulting in information explosion and interdisciplinary approach to research during the second half of the 20th Century. These developments generated new demands and pressures on the services offered by the libraries and Information Centres in our country and elsewhere.

The rapid strides our country made in different spheres of human endeavor since independence and the efforts being made to sustain this progress and reach new heights added new dimensions to the services rendered by LICs. In order to meet these new challenges and find proper, suitable and sustainable solutions and to explore new areas, research has become sine-quo-non in the field of Library and Information Science[1].

Definitions of Research

There are numerous definitions we come across in the english language dictionaries, encyclopedias and other reference tools. But the definition obtained from *The Webster's Third New International Dictionary* is very precise and throws more light on the essential qualities of research. It defined research as "Studious inquiry or examination; especially critical and exhaustive investigation or experimentation, having for its aim the discovery of new facts and their correct interpretation, the revision of accepted conclusions, theories, or laws in the light of newly discovered facts, or practical application of new or revised conclusions, theories or laws"[2].

In other words research is "the manipulation of things, concepts or symbols for the purpose of generalizing to extend, correct or verify knowledge, whether that knowledge aid in the construction of a theory or in the practice of an art"[3]. In another view, research in any discipline is "any systematic quest for knowledge that is characterized by disciplined inquiry. In the process of conducting research an investigator is concerned with three major activities:

1. The definition of terms,
2. The posing of questions or stating of propositions which incorporate the defined terms in an explanatory fashion, and
3. The testing of propositions or search for answers to exploratory questions"[4].

7.2. NEED FOR RESEARCH IN LIS

Several factors have contributed the need for research in LIS. Briefly these are:

1. Changes in the information scenario in the

country due to socio-economic and technological developments naturally necessitated a fresh look in to the discipline.

2. Research at advanced levels is very essential for the growth and development of LIS as discipline on par with other disciplines at least in the domain of Social Sciences. This is because research activities / programmes can sharpen the existing tools and techniques and help to design new ones. These research activities / programmes help to train the required manpower who can, in turn take up research work for further advancement.
3. In order to find solutions to the problems faced in the management of LICs, the Librarians / Information Officers and other professionals should qualify themselves by obtaining research degrees that will enable them to undertake critical, incisive and exhaustive inquiries concerning LICs.
4. In our country, the University Grants Commission (UGC), the apex body for higher education in the country has been insisting on research qualifications for teachers of LIS and librarians working in senior positions in academic libraries especially in College and University Libraries.
5. For recruitment to senior positions in special and technical libraries and information centres, the employers also insist on research degree as an addition qualification from the candidates.
6. From the later part of the 20th century, possessing research degrees in LIS have become essential to acquire position, status, recognition, prestige and also financial benefits.

7. Possessing research degrees / qualifications provide intellectual satisfaction and also satisfy personal vanity.
8. In order to get the same pay scales and status as those of LIS teachers, the library professionals working in College and University libraries must acquire similar research qualifications.
9. Possessing research degrees, and the experience gained in the pursuit of research may enhance the intellectual levels and capacity of the professionals and thereby enable them to provide better and improved library and information services to the user community. In the case of LIS teachers research experience help them to enhance quality of teaching and publication activity and guide the students in their research endeavour.[5, 6]

7.3. OBSTACLES IN LIS RESEARCH

Prof. Krishan Kumar has identified the following barriers or obstacles to research in LIS.[7, 8]

1. "Almost an apathy on the part of our profession towards research. The profession has certainly not provided enough recognition or encouragement to research achievements.
2. Not only lack of interest in research process, but also a strong indifference to the results of research. Libraries themselves hardly care about the results of research. Besides disinterest, there is often distrust or hostility towards research as well as research process and results.
3. Communication of research results is not satisfactory. There is scope for improvement in this context.

4. There is lack of research tradition. In many countries, research in L&IS is a recent phenomenon, with the result, there is lack of tradition. However, in USA, the tradition goes back to 1930s.
5. In developing countries, there is lack of financial support, facilities, documents, secretarial assistance, etc. Developed countries are much better off in this regard.
6. L & IS Faculty is expected to participate actively in academic (Committee work, carrying out research, teaching, etc) and professional activities and also provide leadership to the profession. This can be highly demanding.
7. Often faculty may not possess research degrees and may not have undertaken serious research; as a consequence, they may not be in a position to guide research adequately.
8. Often, librarians do not maintain proper data required for research or they do not extend cooperation in providing the same due to laziness or fear of getting exposed. This can prove to be handicap".

Rajya Laksshmi[9] identified the following factors inhibiting rapid research in LIS field:

1. "Small size of LIS faculities in LIS Schools and their heavy work load,
2. Lack of research qualifications,
3. Lack of financial support in the form of research fellowships or scholarships for young people to work on full time basis.
4. Lack of proper library facilities.
5. Non-availability of the essential data from libraries and parent organizations.

6. Non-availability of research supervisors for topics involving inters- disciplinary research.

Some of the above barriers (obstacles) may be subjective and may not stand for scrutiny. It was true that research in LIS in India started in the 1950s thanks to Dr. S. R. Ranganathan's efforts. But later on research activity in LIS in the Indian Universities accelerated. Many LIS teachers and LIS professionals started doing research to improve their academic and professional qualifications so as to climb up the ladder for higher positions in their career. There are better opportunities now available for youngsters to pursue research in LIS. Facilities are also available in the LIS Departments of Indian Universities to pursue research. Funding agencies, especially, the UGC is offering Junior / Senior Research Fellowship to pursue research in LIS.

7.4. GENESIS OF LIS RESEARCH IN INDIA

The genesis and development of LIS Research in India may be traced back to 1924 when Dr. S. R. Ranganathan appeared on the scene. His seminal contributions to various facets of librarianship, initially, later Library and Information Science enriched the discipline and transformed it from Art into Science. He was primarily responsible for introducing University level Courses in our Country after independence.

At present there are about 100 Universities in the Country having LIS Departments, some of them are full-fledged offering BLISc / MLISc / MLIS (Two Year Integrated) Courses. More than ninty Universities have introduced research courses leading to the award of M.Phil / Ph.D. programmes. These are in addition to Open and Distance Learning Universities, Institutes of Correspondence Education of traditional universities offering LIS Course at different levels. Some of the Open Universities like IGNOU, New Delhi and Dr. B. R. A. O. U., Hyderabad have also introduced M.Phil and Ph.D. programmes. The credit of introducing a Doctoral Programme in LIS for the first time in the Country goes to Dr. S. R. Ranganathan. He introduced the programme in 1950 at the University of Delhi. Dr. D. B. Krishna Rao was the first scholar to obtain Ph.D. Degree in LIS from the University of Delhi in 1957, under the abele and scholarly guidance of Dr. S. R. Ranganathan. The topic for his doctoral research was *"Facet Analysis and Depth Classification of Agriculture"*.

For nearly two decades, no other University in the Country seems to have either introduced Ph.D. programme or conferred a PhD. Degree in LIS. It was turn of Panjab University, Chandigarh which produced the second Ph.D. scholar in India. Dr. Pandey S. K. Sharma obtained Ph.D. in LIS in 1977 from this University under the supervision of Dr. J.S. Sharma. His research topic was *"Expansion and Modification of DDC (18th Edition) for Classifying Indological Books with special reference to Indian Philosophy & Indian Relgion"*[10]. It is pertinent to note that both the Ph.D. theses deal with Library Classification which occupied prominent place in curricula of LIS Schools during the 1960s and 1970s. In between these two decades, Satija observed that "Some librarians got Ph.D.s by working in some other Departments on Library Science or fringe fields. In the meantime many universities such as Bangalore, BHU, Rajasthan, Delhi, Gulbarga, Karnatak have produced varying number of doctorates ... As many as 30 Universities have doctoral programmes though many of them are yet produce any Ph.D."[11]

Quality of LIS Research

The 1970s saw slow growth in the expansion of LIS research in India. However, the situation changed during the 1980s and 1990s and there has been rapid increase in the number of M.Phil and Ph.D. degrees awarded by the Library Schools. But this trend indirectly affects the quality of LIS research in India. Mangla observed that "The increase has certainly affected adversely the quality of research work currently done and has created an urgent need for proper scrutiny and control of research under taken in Library Schools around the country"[12]. To assess the quality of a research work Satija[12-A] identified the following criteria.

"1. How many papers based on the research have been published in reference and international journals?
2. How many dissertations have been published as independent and readable books?
3. How may times such a research work has been quoted or cited in text books or other derivative works or collateral research?
4. It would be too much to ask if any patent has been granted on the research work."

Progressively LIS research accelerated in due course and reached appreciable heights by the end of the 20th century and same is being continued at the beginning of the 21st Century.

7.5. NUMBER OF PH.DS AWARDED

There were no authentic figures available to study and analyze the subject wise distribution of Ph.Ds in LIS awarded by the Indian Universities. Professional Journals in LIS and Newsletters brought out by professional associations such as: IASLIC, ILA, IATLIS report the award of Ph.Ds in LIS from time to time. *University News* being published by Association of Indian Universities reports the award of Ph.D. degrees in LIS from time to time under the heading *Theses of the Month.* Besides these sources attempts have been made to compile a bibliography of doctoral theses awarded by the Indian Universities by P.S.G. Kumar[13,14], R. S. R. Varalakshmi[15], Devraj Singh[16]. Prabha Verma and N. L. Shailaja[17] have also compiled Bibliography of Doctoral Theses in Library and Information Science in India and presented the list alphabetically by subject. There is no time frame for this bibliography and lists 292 theses awarded by the Indian Universities. There are others who have attempted to compile bibliography or list of doctoral theses subject wise, region wise, university wise and State wise. But the figures arrived at by these aforesaid attempts fail to provide true or correct figures as to the number of Ph.Ds awarded in LIS in a given time frame.

R. S. R. Varalakshmi arrived at figure of 180 awarded during the years 1950 and 1993 (up to April). The year wise break up was as follows:

Year	No.of Ph.Ds	Year	No.of Ph.Ds
1950	1	1982	2
1954	1	1983	9
1957	1	1984	18
1963	1	1985	20
1966	1	1986	5
1972	1	1987	8
1973	1	1988	8
1977	4	1989	17
1978	3	1990	14
1979	2	1991	15
1980	2	1992	33
1981	3	1993(Upto April)	5
		Total	180

She also analyzed these 180 theses on the basis of Subject and the relevant Table is given below:[18]

Sl. No.	Subject		No. of Ph.Ds.	%age
1	Communication and Libraries		05	02.27
2	LIS Activities			
	Buildings	03	59	32.77
	Planning and Management	32		
	Preservation	02		
	Professional & Professionals	13		
	Application of Information Technologies	10		
3	Information Storage and Retrieval			
	Cataloging / Indexing	09	22	
	Classification	11		
	Knowledge	02		
4	Dissemination of Information			
	Information Services	06	39	21.66
	Information Systems	06		
	Reading Interests	04		
	User Studies	16		
	Bibliographies	03		
	Cooperation	04		
5	Education for Library & Information Science		04	02.22
6	Biblio-metric Studies		16	08.88
7	Literature Studies		10	06.66
	Children's' Literature		02	
8	Archives		02	01.11
9	Development of Libraries		15	08.33
10	LI Services in other Countries		06	03.33
	Total:		180	99.95%

Dev Raj Sharma[19] compiled bibliography of "Doctoral Research in Library and Information Science in Indian Universities" covering the period 1950-1997. The entries are arranged alphabetically by the name of the Research Scholar. The alphabetical part is well supported by: *(a) Subject Index, (b) Advisor Index, (c) University Index, and (d) Chronology Index.* The bibliography lists a total of 339 theses. The compiler opined that "although all the theses are not submitted after pursuing research in the Departments of Library and Information Science, but these are directly related to topics in the field of Library Science". Each entry provides, in addition to the name of the research scholar, title of the thesis, degree awarded such as Ph.D. / D.Phil / D.Litt. etc., the year of submission / award of degree in circular brackets ( ) followed by the name of the University / Institution to which the thesis was submitted and finally the name of the Advisor (Supervisor / Guide).

P.S.G. Kumar[20] in his article provided chronological distribution of doctorates awarded to library professionals between the years 1950 and 1997. A total of 293 doctorates were awarded during this period. The chronological breakup was as follows:

Sl. No.	Year:	No. of Doctorates Awarded	Sl.No.	Year:	No. of Doctorates Awarded
1	1950	01	16	1985	15
2	1951	01	17	1986	10
3	1952	01	18	1987	06
4	1954	01	19	1988	08
5	1957	01	20	1989	24
6	1966	02	21	1990	09
7	1972	01	22	1991	29
8	1973	05	23	1992	48
9	1977	06	24	1993	11
10	1978	02	25	1994	29
11	1979	04	26	1995	23
12	1980	07	27	1996	13
13	1981	02	28	1997	07
14	1982	12	**Total:**	**293**	
15	1984	15			

He has also provided the subject wise breakup of doctorates in LIS which was as follows:

Sl. No.	**Area:**	**No.**	**Sl. No.**	**Area:**	**No.**
1	Anthropology	01	10	Libraries	
2	History	02		—Academic	07
3	Library and Information Science			—Children's	01
	—Archives	02		—Medical	01
	—Automation	09		—National	02
	—Bibliography	05		—Public	11
	—Bibliometric Studies	11		—Special	09
	—Citation Analysis	07		—University	20
	—Cataloguing	02	11	Management	
	—Classification	11		—General	04
	—Documentation	03		—Financial	06
	—Indexing	12		—Personnel	10
	—Indic Names	01		—Manuscripts	02
	—Information Needs	06	12	Non-book Material	01
	—Networking	02	13	Other Areas: Literature	
	—Retrieval	02		—English	01
	—Services	15		—Hindi	06
	—Systems	02		—Sanskrit	01
	—Technology	14		—Kannada	01
04	Knowledge	05		—Urdu	01
05	Preservation	03	14	Scientometric Studies	02
06	Reading Habits	03	15	Periodical List	08
07	Reference Literature	05	16	Political Science	02
08	User Studies	09	17	Religion	
09	Library			—Budhism	01
	—Building	03		—Christanity	01
	—Education	10		—Islam	01
	—History	04	18	Science	
	—Legislation	06		—Chemistry	01
	—Movement	05		—Pharmacology	01
	—Profession	14		—Sociology	04
	—Use	06			
	—Networking	08		Total:	293

According to S. C. Biswas the "INFLIBNET database listed nearly 600 Ph.D. theses on LIS from 53 Universities (listed 1029 theses including several incomplete and duplicate entries). Both Kumar and INFLIBNET stated categorically, the data on LIS Doctoral Degree are incomplete due to lack of complete support from Universities"[21]. He further states that "INFLIBNET claimed to have received data mostly online, in creating data base (for LIS) covering the period 1980-2008"[22].

A. A. N. Raju has been compiling since 1993, bibliography of theses presented to Indian Universities for the award of Ph.D. degrees in Library and Information Science and as reported mainly in *University News*, the official organ of Association of Indian Universities (AIU) and other sources. The following table provides figures for the years 1993-2012 i.e. a span of 20 years which accounts for 755 doctorates awarded.

Year	No. of Doctorates Awarded	Year	No. of Doctorates Awarded
1993	19	1994	20
1995	24	1996	13
1997	25	1998	16
1999	42	2000	31
2001	36	2002	33
2003	59	2004	60
2005	44	2006	55
2007	58	2008	48
2009	50	2010	51
2011	39	2012	32
Total			755

The above Table shows that during the years 2003 and 2004 highest number of 59 and 60 doctorates respectively for each year had been awarded followed by 58 in 2007, 55 in 2006, 51 in 2010 and 50 in 2009. The appended Table provides figures for broad subject wise breakup of doctorates in LIS from 1993-2012.

Bairam Khan and Amit Kumar Das[23] compiled figures on the award of Ph.Ds in LIS by the Universities in India between the years 1957 and 2010 as reported in *University News*. According to these two authors at total of 864 Ph.Ds were awarded by the Indian Universities. The following Table provides year wise breakup of number of Ph.Ds awarded:

Table

Year	No. of Ph.Ds awarded	Year	No. of Ph.Ds awarded
1957	1	1963	1
1966	1	1968	0
1972	2	1973	1
1976	0	1977	4
1978	3	1979	2
1980	4	1981	4
1982	3	1983	11
1984	13	1985	21
1986	18	1987	12
1988	9	1990	18
1991	32	1992	51
1993	38	1994	36
1995	38	1996	36
1997	21	1998	22
1999	33	2000	30
2001	20	2002	33
2003	49	2004	46
2005	52	2006	30
2007	46	2008	39
2009	26	2010	36
		Total:	**864**

Table : Broad subjectwise breakup of doctorates in LIS awarded by Indian Universities from 1993-2012 i.e. for a period of 20 years

Name of the broad subject field	YEARS																				Total
	1993	1994	1995	1996	1997	1998	1999	2000	2001	2002	2003	2004	2005	2006	2007	2008	2009	2010	2011	2012	
Academic Libraries	-	-	-	-	-	-	2	-	1	4	2	-	-	3	2	1	-	-	2	2	19
Archival Libraries	-	-	-	-	-	-	-	-	-	1	-	-	-	-	-	-	-	-	-	-	01
Bibliographies/Bio-bibliography	-	-	-	-	-	-	-	-	-	-	-	1	2	1	1	-	1	-	-	-	06
Bibliometrics / Informatics / Scientometrics	-	2	1	1	3	-	3	5	-	1	2	4	7	1	5	9	1	3	2	2	52
Cataloguing	1	1	1	1	1	-	1	--	-	-	1	-	-	-	1	-	-	-	-	-	08
Citation Analysis	-	-	-	-	3	-	-	-	4	-	-	-	1	1	1	3	-	-	-	-	13
College Libraries	-	-	-	-	-	-	2	1	1	1	-	5	1	1	1	4	2	2	3	3	27
Communication	-	-	-	-	-	-	-	-	-	-	-	1	-	-	2	-	-	-	1	-	04
Community Information	-	-	1	-	-	-	1	3	-	1	-	1	-	-	1	-	1	-	-	-	09
Computerization	1	-	1	-	-	-	-	-	-	-	3	3	2	1	3	-	3	1	-	-	18
Databases	-	-	-	-	-	1	-	1	2	-	-	-	-	-	-	1	-	-	-	-	05
Government libraries	1	-	-	-	-	-	-	-	-	2	-	-	-	-	-	2	-	-	-	-	05
Indexing Systems	1	-	1	-	-	-	-	1	-	-	1	1	2	-	-	-	-	1	2	-	10
Information Centres / Services	-	-	1	-	1	-	3	1	1	2	2	2	-	7	4	5	6	3	2	1	41
Information Systems	3	2	5	2	2	1	4	1	2	-	4	2	2	1	-	-	-	2	2	1	36
Information Storage / Retrieval	-	-	-	-	-	1	4	-	-	-	1	1	2	-	-	1	1	-	-	-	08
Information Technology and Allied Fields	-	-	-	-	1	-	1	-	4	3	8	9	5	7	8	2	10	4	5	4	71
LIS Education / Research / Training	-	-	-	-	-	2	-	2	4	1	-	1	-	-	2	2	-	4	-	-	18

Table Contd...

Library Associations / Profession	2	-	1	-	-	-	-	-	-	-	-	-	-	-	-	-	-	3	-	-	06
Library Buildings	-	-	-	-	-	-	-	-	-	2	-	-	-	-	-	-	-	-	-	-	02
Library Classification	-	-	-	-	-	-	2	1	2	-	2	-	-	-	-	-	1	1	-	-	09
Library Collections	-	-	-	-	-	-	-	-	1	-	4	2	2	10	4	2	2	7	5	2	41
Library History / Library Movement	-	-	-	-	-	-	1	1	-	-	1	1	-	-	-	-	-	-	-	-	04
Library Legislation	-	-	-	-	1	-	-	-	-	-	-	-	-	-	-	1	-	1	-	-	03
Library Management	1	2	2	2	5	3	5	3	1	2	2	4	5	2	1	2	-	1	2	4	49
Library Software	-	-	-	-	-	-	1	-	-	-	-	-	-	-	1	-	1	1	-	-	04
Marketing of Information / products	-	1	-	-	-	-	1	-	-	1	1	3	2	1	1	-	-	1	-	1	13
Mass Media	-	-	-	-	-	-	-	-	-	-	-	-	-	-	-	3	1	-	-	-	04
National Libraries	-	-	1	-	-	1	-	-	--	-	-	-	-	-	-	-	-	-	-	-	02
Networking / Resource Sharing	-	1	-	-	1	1	2	2	1	2	2	4	2	3	1	-	5	1	-	-	28
Non-book Materials	-	-	-	-	-	-	1	-	-	-	1	-	-	-	-	-	-	-	-	-	02
Public Library System / Public Libraries	1	2	1	3	1	-	1	-	-	2	3	-	-	-	8	2	4	4	-	-	35
Reference and Information tools and sources	1	1	-	-	1	-	1	-	-	-	-	1	-	1	-	-	1	-	-	-	07
School Libraries	-	1	-	-	-	-	-	-	-	-	-	1	-	1	-	-	-	1	-	-	04
Special Libraries	1	-	-	1	-	-	2	1	1	-	4	-	2	5	2	-	-	2	1	2	25
University Libraries	3	3	4	-	2	-	5	3	2	3	11	7	1	3	3	7	-	1	7	2	67
User Study / User Education	4	3	4	3	3	6	2	5	9	4	4	6	6	3	5	6	7	6	5	8	99
Total:	19	20	24	13	25	16	42	31	36	33	59	60	44	55	58	48	50	51	39	32	755

Sources: ***University News, IASLIC Newsletter, IATLIS Communication*** and ***ILA Newsletter.***

There is no agreement as to the total figures arrived at by P.S.G. Kumar and Dev Raj Sharma as for both of them, the time frame was 1950-1997. For the said period Dev Raj Sharma arrived at the figure 339, where as P.S.G. Kumar arrived at the figure 293. Similarly the figure arrived at by R. S. R. Varalakshmi stands at 180 for the period 1950-1993 (up to April). Likewise the figures arrived at by Khan and Das stand at 864 between the years 1957 and 2010.

7.6. SOME OBSERVATIONS

During the 20 year period i.e. 1993-2012, the highest number of theses i.e. 99 were submitted on User Study / Education followed by 71 on Information Technology (IT) and allied disciplines, 67 on University Libraries, 52 on Bibliometrics / Informetrics / Scientometrics, and 49 on Library Management. Various facets of User Study / Education have become favorite topics for research scholars to undertake research as it appears to be 'soft' and amenable topic for carrying out research both for the Research Scholar and Research Supervisor / Guide to guide the Research Scholars. The advent of Information Technology had a greater impact on the Research Scholars to undertake research on various facets of IT including Internet, Digital Libraries and Virtual Libraries. Various facets of University Libraries had been another favorite broad subject field chosen by the Research Scholars to pursue research. Bibliometrics / Informetrics / Scientometrics had been the next favorite broad subject field for Research Scholars to undertake research in the Indian Universities. The year 2008 saw the highest number of 9 theses submitted than any other year between 1993 and 2012. This was followed by 'Library Management' of which various facets of Library Management were selected for pursuing research.

Theses Presentation in Indian Languages

There are instances where some universities allowed the Research Scholars to present their theses in Indian languages such as: Hindi, Marathi, Gujarathi and Bengali. In the year 2006 1 thesis in Hindi, 2 in Gujarati and 2 in Marathi were submitted for adjudication. Likewise in the year 2007, 1 in Hindi and 1 in Bengali were submitted. In the year 2008, 1 in Marathi and 1 in Hindi were submitted. In the year 2010, 3 in Hindi were submitted for adjudication.

Presentation of doctoral theses in Indian languages in LIS may restrict adjudication by the examiners to a particular geographical area. This may indirectly affect the quality of the theses and restrict its wider circulation to a larger community of researchers and adjudicators. If they are published, the readership shall be very much restricted to that particular language group. This trend was not yet percolated down to Southern States of India[24].

Research Supervisors / Guides

The Universities in India follow different rules / guidelines to recognize Supervisors / Guides for guiding doctoral research scholars. If one crosses 65 years age he/she is not eligible to guide doctoral research. Also there is a stipulation that a particular supervisor cannot guide more than six scholars at a time. During the 70s, 80s and 90s of the twentieth century, there was dearth of Research Supervisors. Now the situation has been slowly changing for the better. Now we find a good number of Research Supervisors to guide the doctoral students in majority of LIS Departments in the Country. Some of them are young and dynamic.

Joint Research Supervisors / Guides

It is not uncommon to have Joint Research

Supervisors / to guide doctoral research scholars. There are several instances where a particular research scholar had been guided by joint supervisors. But there should be perfect understanding between the Joint Supervisors and a good rapport with the Research Scholar. There should not be personality clashes or differences among the Research Supervisors and their differences, if any, should not harm the progress of research endeavor of the Research Scholar. It should not be neither riding two horses nor dragging into different directions. The analysis of doctoral theses during the period 2006 and 2010 revealed that there were instances of joint supervisors guiding research scholars.

The following Table provides the List of Joint Supervisors.

Table: Joint Research Supervisors

2006	2007	2008	2009	2010
1. Dr. TAV Murthy And Prof. MTM Khan	1. Dr.TAV Murthy And Prof. MTM Khan	1. Dr. B.K. Sharma And Dr. Hemant Sharma	1. Dr. P. Hangsingh And Prof. A.S. Chandel	1. Dr. K. Nityanandam And Dr. R. Raju
2. Prof. S. Kumar And Dr. D. B. K. Sharma	2. Dr. Pandey S.K. Sharma And Prof. MTM Khan	2. Dr. B. K. Sharma And Dr. Hemant Sharma	2. Dr. P. Hangsingh And Prof. A. S. Chandel	2. Dr. S. Mustafa And Dr. K. Q. Zaidi
3. Prof. P. Barua And Dr. C.R. Sain	3. Prof. Bijoypada Mukharjee And Prof. J.K. Sarkel		3. Dr. M.B. Bankapur And Dr. S.L. Sangam	3. Prof. Rita Sinha And Dr. Mohanlal
	4. Dr. Biplab Chakraborthy And Dr. Soumitra Sarkar		4. Dr. B.K. Sharma And Dr. Hemant Sharma	
	5. Prof.Probir Roy Choudhury And Prof. J.K. Sarkel			

There are many more examples of Joint Supervision for guidance of Students of doctoral research in LIS. There are few examples of guides from other subject fields associated in LIS research, where interdisciplinary nature of the research topic is involved.

REFERENCES

1. Raju, A. A. N. A Look into LIS Research in India during the past five years. *In* Fifty Years of Library and Information Science Education in India. *Ed.* by A. A. N. Raju *etal.* Hyderabad, IATLIS, 1997. P.186.
2. Websters" Third New International Dictionary. V2. London, Bell, 1964. P.1930.
3. Encyclopedia of Social Sciences. 13. London, Macmillan, 1942. P.330.
4. Encyclopedia of Library and Information Science. V25. New York, Marcel Dekker, 1978. P.254.
5. Raju, A. A. N. A Look into LIS Research.... *Opcit.* P.187.
6. Krishan Kumar and Sardana, J.L. Research in Library and Information Science in Indian Library Schools. *In* Library and Information Science Education in India. Delhi, MacMillan, 1981. Pp.122-139.
7. Krishan Kumar. Research Methods in Library and Information Science. New Delhi, Har-Anand Publications, 1992. P.13.
8. Krishan Kumar and Sardana J.L. Research in Library and Information Science... *opcit.*
9. Rajyalakshmi, D. Library Science Education at Cross Roads in India. *In* Information Technology and its impact on LIS education and Management. Ed. by A. A. N. Raju, *etal.* Hyderabad, Delta Publishing House, 1997. P.6.
10. Raju, A. A. N. Library and Information Science Research in India. *In* Academic Libraries: Role in National Development. *Ed.* by Dorothy Isaac *etal.* Madras, T. R. Publications, 1993. P.16.
11. Satija, M.P. Garnering the fruits of research: Sources of Indian LIS Dissertations. *In* Library and Information Science in India. New Delhi, Sterling, 1992. P.102.

12. Mangla, P. B. Library and Information Science Education: Trends and Issues. *In* 50 years of LIS in India. Delhi, Shipra Publications, 1998. P.291.

12A. Satija, M.P. What Ails Doctoral Research in Library and Information Science. *DESIDOC J. Lib. Inf. Tech.* V 30, N5, 2010. Pp. 61-66.

13. Kumar, PSG. Doctoral Studies in Library and Information Science. New Delhi, Concept, 1987.

14. Kumar, PSG. Doctoral Studies in Library and Information Science in India: A Study. *DESIDOC Bulletin of Information Technology,* V18, N1, January 1998. Pp.5-10.

15. Varalakshmi, R. S. R. Library and Information Science in India: Subject Perspective. *Library Science...* V31, 1994. Paper J. Pp.91-110.

16. Sharma, Devraj. Doctoral Research in Library and Information Science in Indian Universities. Palampur, The Author, 1997. P48.

17. Verma, Prabha and Shailaja, N.L. Bibliography of Doctoral Theses in Library and Information Science. *DESIDOC Bulletin of Information Technology* V18, N1, January, 1998. Pp.22-24.

18. Varalakshmi, R.S.R. Library and Information Science in India... *opcit.* P.5.

19. Sharma, Devraj. Doctoral Research in Library and Information Science...*opcit.* P.5.

20. Kumar, PSG. Doctoral Studies in Library Science... *opcit.* Pp.5-10

21. Biswas, Subhas C. Library and Information Science Research Landscape in India. *IASLIC Bulletin.* V54, N4, December 2010. P.206.

22. Ibid. P.213.

23. Khan, Bairam and Das, Anant Kumar. LIS Research in India with Special Reference to West Bengal: A Trend. *In* LIS Education, Research and Training: Vision 2020. IATLISs 2011. Patiala, DLISc, Panjabi University, 2011. Pp.339-251.

24. Raju, A. A. N. An Analysis of Doctoral Theses in L IS accepted by the Indian Universities during the past five years (2006-2010). *In* LIS Education, Research and Training: Vision 2020. IATLIS 2011. Patiala, DLISc, Panjabi University, 2011. Pp.285-291.

ANNEXURE

The University Grants Commission (UGC), the apex body for general higher education in the country has formulated the minimum standards and procedure for the award of M.Phil / Ph.D. degrees under regulation 2009 and the said regulation was circulated to all the Universities i.e., Central, State and Deemed to be Universities in the Country through its circular letter in August 2009 for guidance and compliance. The said regulation is reproduced below for ready reference.

UNIVERSITY GRANTS COMMISSION

UGC (MINIMUM STANDARDS AND PROCEDURE FOR AWARDS OF M.PHIL/Ph.D DEGREE)

REGULATION, 2009

New Delhi 110002, the 1st June 2009

F. 1-1/2009 (PS) Exemp.-In exercise of the powers conferred by clause (e) & (g) of Sub-section (1) of Section 26 of University Grants Commission Act, 1956 (3 of 1956), the University Grants Commission hereby makes the following regulations, namely :-

Short Title, Application and Commencement:

1. These regulations may be called University Grants Commission (Minimum Standards and Procedure for award of M.Phil/Ph.D. Degree), Regulations 2009.

2. They shall apply to every University established or incorporated by or under a Central Act, Provincial Act or a State Act, every Institution including a constituent or an affiliated College recognized by the Commission, in consultation with the University concerned under clause (1) of Section 2 of the University Grants Commission Act, 1956, and every Institution deemed to be a

University under section 3 of the said Act.

3. They shall come into force with effect from the date of their publication in the Gazette of India.
4. All Universities, Institutions, Deemed to be Universities and Colleges/Institutions of National Importance shall be eligible for conducting M.Phil and Ph.D. Programmes.
5. Notwithstanding anything contained in these \Regulations or any other Rule or regulation, for the time being in force, no University, Institution, Deemed to be University and College/Institution of National Importance shall conduct M.Phil and Ph.D. Programmes through distance education mode.

ELIGIBILITY CRITERIA FOR M.PHL/PH.D. SUPERVISOR

6. All Universities, Institutions, Deemed to be Universities and Colleges / Institutions of National Importance shall lay down the criteria for the faculty to be recognized as Research Supervisor both for M.Phil and Ph.D. Programmes.
7. All Universities, Institutions, Deemed to be Universities and Colleges / Institutions of National Importance shall lay down and decide on Annual Basis, a predetermined and manageable number of M.Phil and doctoral students depending on the number of the available eligible Faculty Supervisors. A Supervisor shall not have, at any given point of time, more than Eight Ph.D. Scholars and Five M.Phil. Scholars.
8. The number of seats for M.Phil and Ph.D. shall

be decided well in advance and notified din the University Website or advertisement. All Universities, Institutions, Deemed to be Universities and Colleges / Institutions of National Importance shall widely advertise the number of available seats for M.Phil / Ph.D. studies and conduct admission on regular basis.

PROCEDURE FOR ADMISSION

9. (i) All Universities, Institutions, Deemed to be Universities and Colleges / Institutions of National Importance shall admit M.Phil Doctoral students through an Entrance Test conducted at the level of individual University, Institutions, Deemed to be Universality, College / Institution of National Importance. The University may decide separate terms and conditions for those students who qualify UGC / CSIR (JRF) Examination/SLET/GATE/teacher fellowship holder or have passed M.Phil Programme for Ph.D. Entrance Test. Similar approach may be adopted in respect of Entrance Rest for M.Phil Programme.

   (ii) It shall be followed by an interview to be organized by the School/ Department/ Institution/University as the case may be.

   (iii) At the time of interview, doctoral candidates are expected to discuss their research interest/area.

   (iv) Only the predetermined number of students may be admitted to M.Phil/Ph.D. programme.

10. The admission to the Ph.D. Programme would be either directly or through M.Phil Programme.

11. While granting admission to students to M.Phil/ Ph.D.programmes, the Department/Institute/ School will pay due attention to the National/ State Reservation Policy.

ALLOCATION OF SUPERVISOR

12. The allocation of the supervisor for a selected student shall be decided by the Department in a formal manner depending on the number of student per faculty member, the available specialization among the faculty supervisors, and the research interest of the student as indicated during interview by the student. The allotment/ allocation of supervisor shall not be left to the individual student or teacher.

COURSE WORK

13. After having been admitted, each M.Phil/PhD. Student shall be required by the Universities, Institutions, and Deemed to be Universities and Colleges/Institutions of National Importance, as the case may be to undertake course work for a minimum period of one semester. The Course work shall be treated as pre M.Phil/Ph.D. preparation and must include a course on research methodology which may include quantitative methods and Computer Applications. It may also involve reviewing of published research in the relevant field. The individual Universities, Institutions, Deemed to be Universities and Colleges/Institutions of National Importance, as the case may be, shall decide the minimum qualifying requirement for allowing a student to proceed further with the writing of the dissertation. If found necessary, course work may

be carried out by doctoral candidates in sister Departments / Institutes either within or outside the University for which due credit will be given to them.

EVALUATION AND ASSESSMENT METHODS

14. Upon satisfactory completion of course work and research methodology, which shall form part & parcel of M.Phil/Ph.D. Programme, the M.Phil/Ph.D. Scholar shall undertake research work and produce a draft thesis within a reasonable time, as stipulated by the Institution concerned.
15. Prior to submission of the thesis, the student shall make a pre-M.Phil/Ph.D. presentation in 'the Department' that may be open to all faculty members and research students, for getting feedback and comments, which may be suitably incorporated into the draft thesis under the advice of the supervisor.
16. Ph.D. candidates shall publish one research paper in a referred Journal before the submission of the thesis/monograph for adjudication, and produce evidence for the same in the form of acceptance letter or the reprint.
17. The thesis produced by the M.Phil/Ph.D. student in the Institutions/Departments and submitted to the University, Institution, Deemed to be University, College/Institution of National Importance, as the case may be, shall be evaluated by at least two experts, our of which at least one shall be from outside the State. It shall be up to the University, Institution, Deemed to be University, College/Institution of National Importance concerned to have one examiner from outside the Country.

18. On receipt of satisfactory evaluation reports, M.Phil/Ph.D. students shall undergo a viva voce examination which shall also be open defended.

DEPOSITORY WITH UGC

19. Following the successful completion of the evaluation process and announcements of the award of M.Phil/Ph.D., the University shall submit a soft copy of the M.Phil/Ph.D. thesis to be UGC within a period of thirty days, for hosting the same in INFLIBNET, accessible to all Institutions/Universities.
20. Along with the Degree, the Degree awarding University, Institution Deemed to be University, College/Institution of National Importance, as the case may be, shall issue a Provisional Certificate certifying to the effect that the Degree has been awarded in accordance with the provisions to these Regulations of the UGC.

All most all the Universities in the Country have formulated their own M.Phil/Ph.D. Rules and Regulations keeping in view of the M.Phil/Ph.D. regulation formulated by the UGC. For example Osmania University, Hyderabad, one of the oldest Universities in the Country, had formulated an elaborate and detailed "Ph.D. Rules and Regulations" for offering and managing research courses like M.Phil / PhD. These rules and regulations include among other things:

1. Procedure for admission into Ph.D.,
2. Ph.D. Eligibility Test,
3. Notification of vacant seats,
4. Ph.D. admission interview,
5. Research Supervisors,

6. Number of candidates allotment to research supervisor,
7. Categories of Ph.D. research Scholars,
8. Ph.D. Course Work and Pre-Ph.D. Examination,
9. Pre-Ph.D. examination and Evaluation of Answer Scripts,
10. Change of Jurisdiction,
11. Progress Reports,
12. Seminar Presentation,
13. Modification of topic of research and title of Ph.D. thesis,
14. Extension of Registration,
15. Publication of a research paper,
16. Cancellation of Ph.D. admission / Registration,
17. Submission of Ph.D. thesis,
18. Ph.D. thesis evaluation / adjudication,
19. Ph.D. Viva-voce Examination and
20. Declaration of Ph.D. Result.

Ph.D. Course Work

The Ph.D. Course Work shall comprise of two theory papers as follows: *Paper-1: Research Methodology*. Common to all the candidates admitted in a Department (consisting 100 Marks). The syllabus of the Paper consists of research techniques / methods of the concerned subject. *Paper-2: Broad Field of Specialization* (100 Marks). The Syllabus of this Paper consists of current concepts / trends in the specialization of the subject. This examination shall be conducted for the admitted candidates after one semester Ph.D. Course Work.

As an example the syllabus of *Paper-1: Research*

Methodology and *Paper-2: Broad Field of Specialization* framed by the Department of Library and Information Science, Osmania University, Hyderabad is given below for information.

Ph.D. SYLLABUS 2010-11

PPAPER-1: RESEARCH METHODOLOGY

Unit-1: ***Research***

Definition, need and purpose, Basic Concepts: Validity, Reliability, Objectivity, Subjectivity. Variables: Dependent, Independent and Intervening. Logic: Induction and Deduction. Institution. Scientific method. Trends in LIS Research.

Unit-2: ***Research Design***

Aims and Objectives. Scope and limitations. Problem identification, formulation and statement of the problem.

Hypothesis : Definition. Formulation. Verification.

Unit-3: ***Methods of Research:***

Survey, descriptive, comparative, historical, experimental, case study and Delphi technique.

Unit-4: ***Methods and Tools of Data Analysis:***

Descriptive Statistics – Inferential Statistics: Chisquare test, Measures of dispersion, Central Tendencies.

Unit-5: ***Writing Research Report:***

Structure & Contents of Report, presentation of findings – Graphical Presentation of Data. Style Sheets, Citation of Print, Electronic and Internet Sources.

Statistical Packages – SPSS.

Paper-2 (B): Scientific & Technical Libraries:

1. Scientific & Technical Libraries (Special Libraries): Definition, Objectives, Functions and Services. Development of Special Libraries in India. Organization and Management of Special Libraries. Evaluation of Library Services and Procedures. HR Planning & Performance.
2. Documentation centers, Information centers, Information Analysis / Evaluation Centers, Referral Centers. Data Centers. Information Systems - NISSAT, NISCAIR, DESIDOC, NASSDOC, CORD, SENDOC. National Agricultural Library, National Medical Library, National Science Library of India – their functions and services.
3. Information Communication Methods. IPR, Right to Information Act. Marketing of Information. Digital Libraries: Strategies for Development of Digital Libraries Internet Information Resources and Services. Search & Retrieval Methods. Open Access Resources and their access.
4. Software : Open Source and proprietary software. Digital Library Software (DSpace) Digitization Process. Standards and formats. Subject Gateways, Blogs, Web Directories.
5. Information Storage & Retrieval
   Content Creation and Analysis
   Metadata. OAI-PMH.

8

Ph.D. Output in LIS Departments

As stated, the output of M.Phil and Ph.D. Degrees in LIS has been greatly accelerated since 1970s as many Departments introduced research courses leading to the award of M.Phil and Ph.D. degrees. The insistence of Ph.D. degree for the post of Lecturer (Assistant Professor) by the UGC forced the prospective candidates to obtain Ph.D. degree in LIS and ac celebrated the LIS Departments in the country to introduce M.Phil and Ph.D. programmes for the benefit of the candidates and consequently the award of Ph.D degrees accelerated since 1970s[1].

Some of the LIS Departments of the Universities such as Annamalai, Gwalior, Dharwad, Delhi, Andhra have produced significant number of Ph.Ds in LIS. As per the Table appended, DLISc, Annamalai University, produced 95 Ph.Ds followed by Jiwaji University, Gwalior (93), Karnataka University (82), Andhra University (63), University of Mysore (60) and University of Delhi (59)[2].

The following Table provides the names of LIS Departments listed alphabetically and number of Ph.Ds awarded against each Department with remarks. After the Table, year wise award of Ph.Ds by each Department and with name of the first Ph.D. awardee and the name of the topic for doctoral research is also given. In addition, the names of Research Supervisors or Research Guides and the number of Ph.D. Scholars guided by them are also given in decreasing order. It is evident that in some of the universities in North India, these were presented in Hindi. In Gujarat in some of the universities, the doctoral dissertations were submitted in Gujarati.

Alphabetical list of LIS Departments / Universities with number of Ph.Ds awarded

S. No.	Name of the Department/ University	No.of Ph.Ds Awarded	Remarks:
1	DLISc, Aligarh Muslim University, Aligarh	20	Up to Octo.2013
2	DLISc, Andhra University, Visakhapatnam	63	Up to 2012
3	DLISc, Annamalai University, Annamalai Nagar, Chidambaram	95	Up to August 2013
4	DLISc, Dr. B.R. Ambedkar Open University, Hyderabad	04	Up to August 2013
5	DLISc, Dr. Babasaheb Ambedkar Marathwada University, Aurangabad	34	Up to 2012
6	DLISc, Benaras Hindu University, Varanasi	21	Up to 2010
7	DLISc, Bangalore University, Bangalore	22	Up to 2010
8	DLISc, Calicut University, Calicut	29	Up to 2008
9	DLISc, Gauhati University, Guwahati	34	Up to May 2013
10	DLISc, Gulbarga University, Gulbarga	37	Up to January 2013
11	DLISc, Gurunanak Dev University, Amritsar	28	Up to Sept. 2013
12	DLISc, Hemachandracharya North Gujarat University, Patan	19	Up to 2012
13	DLISc, Jiwaji University, Gwalior	93	Up to Dec. 2013
14	DLISc, Karnatak University, Dharwad	82	Up to Jan. 2013
15	DLISc, Kuvempu University, Shankargatta (Karnataka)	14	Up to 2011

16	DLISc, M. S. University, Baroda	05	Up to 2011
17	DLISc, Mangalore University, Mangalore	20	Up to 2011
18	DLISc, Manipur University, Imphal	05	Up to 2008
19	DLISc, North-East Hill University, Shillong	20	Up to 2012
20	DLISc, Osmania University, Hyderabad	29	Up to 2012
21	DLISc, Panjab University, Chandigarh	27	Up to July 2013
22	DLISc, Panjabi University, Patiala	15	Up to 2012
23	DLIS, Rashtrasant Tukkadoji Maharaj Nagpur University, Nagpur	53	Up to Sept. 2012
24	DLISc, SNDT Women's University, Mumbai	10	Up to August 2013
25	DLISc, Sambalpur University, Burla, Sambalpur	29	Up to 2012
26	DLISc, Sant Gadge Amravati University, Amravati	11	Up to 2011
27	DLISc, Shivaji University, Kolhapur	06	Up to 2007
28	DLISc,Srikrishna Devaraya University, Anantapur	18	Up to July 2013
29	DLISc, Sri Venkateshwara University, Tirupati	43	Up to 2012
30	DLISc, Thakur Ranmat Singh Autonomous College, Rewa	19	Up to 2012
31	DLISc, University of Burdwan, Burdwan	28	Up to August 2013
32	DLISc, University of Delhi,Delhi	59	Up to 2011
33	DLISc, University of Jammu, Jammu	10	Up to 2012
34	DLISc, University of Kashmir, Srinagar	12	Up to 2011
35	DLISc, University of Lucknow, Lucknow	14	Up to 2012
36	DLISc, University of Madras, Chennai	57	Up to August 2013
37	DLISc, University of Mysore, Mysore	60	Up to 2012
38	DLISc, University of Pune, Pune	43	Up to 2008
39	DLISc, Utkal University, Bhubaneshwar	31	Up to 2012
40	DLISc, Swami Ramanand Thirth Maratwada University, Nanded	04	Up to 2012

1. DLISc, Aligarh Muslim University, Aligarh

The Department of Library and Information Science, Aligarh Muslim University, Aligarh awarded first Ph.D. in LIS in the year 2002 to Dr. Habib-ur-Rahman for his doctoral research on the topic

"Teaching of Library Science in Indian Universities: Problems and Prospects" under the Supervision of Prof. S. M. K. Q. Zaidi. Until 2013 the Department has awarded 20 Ph.Ds in LIS. One teacher candidate Dr. Nishat Fatima submitted her doctoral dissertation independently and got Ph.D. in the year 2010 for her research topic titled "Growth, Development and Services of National Agriculture Library, New Delhi, National Medical Library, New Delhi and National Science Library, New Delhi: A Comparative Study". The year wise award of Ph.Ds is presented in the following Table:

Table

Year	No. of Ph.Ds	Year	No. of Ph.Ds
2002	1	2003	-
2004	-	2005	-
2006	1	2007	-
2008	-	2009	2
2010	3	2011	6
1012	2	2013	5
		Total:	20

Among the Supervisors Prof. S.M.K.Q.Zaidi and Prof. Shabahat Hussain produced 4 Ph.Ds each, followed by Dr. Naushat Ali (3), Dr. M. Moosa Raza (2) and Dr. Nishat Fatima (2), Dr. Sudharma Haridasa (2) and Dr. Mehtab Alam Ansari (2). The largest number of 6 Ph.Ds were awarded in the year 2011 followed by 5 in the year 2013. This Department is a late comer in the domain of LIS Research.

2. DLISc, Andhra University, Visakhapatnam

The Department of Library and Information Science, Andhra University,Visakhapatnam introduced Ph.D. programme in the year 1967 as a special case even though the Department has not yet introduced MLISc programme. Prof. K. Ramakrishna Rao, Professor of Para Psychology who also possessed M.S. in Library Science came forward to guide two faculty members of the Department of LIS – Sri K. Siva Reddy and Sri G. V. S. L. Narasimha Raju. Sri Narasimha Raju did his doctoral research on "Effect of Library Legislation on the Public Library Development in Andhra Pradesh" and obtained Ph.D. degree in the year 1983 and thus becoming the first Ph.Degree holder in LIS not only from the Dept. of LIS, Andhra University, but also the entire State of Andhra Pradesh. Later other Faculty Members and research scholars pursued research and obtained Ph.D. Degrees.

By the end of May 2013, the Department has produced 63 Ph.Ds in LIS. Among the Research Supervisors, Prof. B. Vijayalakshmi produced 10 Ph.Ds followed by Prof. K. Somasekhara Rao (10), Prof. C. Sasikala (8), Prof. R. S. R. Varalakshmi (7), Prof. K. Siva Reddy (6), Prof. P. Soma Raju (6), Prof. G. V. S. L. N. Raju (4) and Prof. P. Bhaskar Rao (4). In respect doctoral research in LIS, the Department is one of leading departments in the country which produced 63 Ph.Ds in LIS. The following Table provides year wise break up of awarded of Ph.Ds.

Table

Year	No. of Ph.Ds	Year	No. of Ph.Ds	Year	No. of Ph.Ds
1983	1	1984	1	1985	1
1986	-	1987	-	1988	-
1989	-	1990	-	1991	1
1992	4	1993	3	1994	5
1995	3	1996	1	1997	1
1998	1	1999	4	2000	2
2001	2	2002	2	2003	2
2004	4	2005	2	2006	3

2007	6	2008	1	2009	4
2010	1	2011	2	2012	5
2013 (Until May 2013)	1			Total	63

3. DLISc, Annamalai University, Chidambaram

Annamalai University, Annamalai Nagar, Chidambaram, is one of the oldest Universities in Tamil Nadu. The DLISc, Annamalai University introduced Ph.D. programe in 1990s and the first Ph.D. was awarded in the year 1990 to Dr.(Ms) Suriya for her doctoral research on the topic "Performance Evaluation of University Libraries in Tamil Nadu: An Application of Cost Effectiveness Analysis" under the guidance of Prof. V. Durairajan. Until August 2003 the Department has produced 95 Ph.Ds which is a record in the award of Ph.Ds in LIS by any Department in the Country. The year wise break up is given in the following Table.

Year	No. of Ph.Ds	Year	No. of Ph.Ds	Year	No. of Ph.Ds
1990	1	1991	-	1992	-
1993	1	1994	-	1995	1
1996	1	1997	-	1998	1
1999	4	2001	1	2002	3
2002	1	2003	6	2004	4
2005	-	2006	5	2007	4
2008	2	2009	4	2010	15
2011	19	2012	12		
2013 (Until Aug. 2013)	8				
Total	**95**				

It is evident from the above Table that from the year 2010 one can notice growth in the number of Ph.Ds awarded. In the year 2011 a record number of

19 Ph.Ds were awarded. Among the Research Guides Dr. M.Nagarajan produced 19 Ph.Ds followed by Dr.M.Suriya (15), Dr. S. Ravi (13), Dr. T. Saravanan (5), Dr. P. Pichappan (5), Dr. M.Aravinthan (5), Dr. S. Mohammad Ismail (5), Dr. M.Sadik Batch (4), Dr. P. Ravichandran (3), Dr. R. Ponnudurai (3), Dr. P. Sivaraman (3), Dr. K. Vijaya kumar (2), Dr. P. Sivaraman (3), Dr. K.Vijaya Kumar (2), and Prof. V. Durairajan (1). Prof. V. Durairajan was the first Professor and Head of the Department and during his stewardship Ph.D. programme was introduced.

4. DLISc, Dr. B. R. Ambedkar Open University, Hyderabad

Dr. B. R. Ambedkar Open University, Hyderabad (A.P.) the first Open University for the entire country introduced M.Phil and Ph.D. programmes in the year 2008. So far the University has produced four Ph.Ds until August 2013. Dr. B. Sattaiah was the first research scholar to obtain Ph.D. in December 2010 who pursued his research on the topic "Use of Information Technology in University Libraries in Andhra Pradesh: A study" under the supervision of Prof. V. Vishwa Mohan. The following Table provides figures for year wise award of Ph.D.s.

Table

Year	No.of Ph.Ds
2010	1
2011	-
2012	2
2013Until Aug.2013	1
Total	4

Two more research scholars have submitted theses in August 2013 and the result is awaited. Among the Research Supervisors Prof. V. Chandrasekhar Rao produced two Ph.Ds followed by Prof. V. Vishwa Mohan (1) and Dr. G. Saroja (1).

5. DLISc, Dr. Babasaheb Ambedkar Maratwada University, Aurangabad

The Department of Library and Information Science, Dr. B. R. Ambedkar Maratwada University was established in the year 1968. BLIS Course was introduced in March / April 1969. MLISc Course was started during the academic year 1985-86. From the year 2002, a two year integrated MLISc Course was started. Research Course leading to the award of Ph.D. was introduced in the 1990s. By the end of the year 2012 the Department produced 34 Ph.Ds in LIS. The first candidate to receive Ph.D. in LIS from this University was Smt. A. A. Vaishnav under the guidance of Prof. N. G. Bapat in the year 1994. She did on the topic "Application of Computer in Library Management". The following Table provides figures for year wise award of Ph.Ds during the years 1994 and 2012.

Table

Year	No. of Ph.Ds	Year	No. of Ph.Ds	Year	No. of Ph.Ds
1994	1	1995	*	1996	1
1997	-	1998	-	1999	-
2000	-	2001	-	2002	3
2003	-	2004	2	2005	3
2006	4	2007	2	2008	2
2009	-	2010	3	2011	8
2012	5				
Total	34				

Among the 34 Ph.D dissertations, four scholars submitted their dissertations in Marathi. Of the

Research Guides, Prof. A. A. Vaishnav produced 16 Ph.Ds, the largest number followed by Dr. S. M. Mohal (6) and Shakuntala Lomte (6). It is pertinent to note that in the year 2008, 8 Ph.Ds were produced than any other year.

6. DLISc, Banaras Hindu University, Varanasi

The Department of Library and Information Science (DLISc), Banaras Hindu University, Varanasi was established in 1941. In the year 1942 the Department introduced Diploma in Library Science, the second of its kind after University of Madras. B.Lib.Sc was introduced in 1961 and M.Lib.Sc during the year 1965, the second of its kind in the country after University of Delhi. A two year integrated MLISc Course was introduced in the year 2005 replacing the existing one year BLISc and one year MLISc Courses. The Department introduced Ph.D. programme in the year 1980. In the year 2008, the Department introduced a new course called PG Diploma in Manuscriptlogy and Palaeography. Later in the year 2011 the said course was upgraded to Masters Degree level and re-designated as M.A. Course in Manuscriptlogy and Palaeography.

Between the year 1982 and 2010 the Department has awarded 21 Ph.Ds in LIS. Sri Sambhunath Singh was the first Research Scholar to be awarded Ph.D. in the year 1982 under the abele guidance of Prof. P. N. Kaula. Dr. S. N. Singh did his doctoral research on the topic "Use of Social Science Literature in India: A Bibliometric Study". The following Table provides figures for the year wise award of Ph.Ds in LIS.

Table

Year	No. of Ph.Ds	Year	No. of Ph.Ds	Year	No. of Ph.Ds
1982	1	1983	1	1984	1
1985	-	1986	-	1987	-
1988	1	1989	1	1990	-
1991	1	1992	1	1993	1
1994	-	1995	1	1996	1
1997	-	1998	-	1999	4
2000	1	2001	-	2002	2
2003	-	2004	-	2005	1
2006	-	2007	1	2010	2
Total	**21**				

Among the Research Guides Prof. H. N. Prasad guided nine Ph.D. scholars followed by Prof. P. N. Kaula (4), Prof. S. N. Singh (4) and Prof. Y. P. Dubey (2). Even though the Department of Library and Information Science is one of the oldest Departments in the Country, the output of Ph.Ds in LIS is not impressive.

7. DLISc, Bangalore University, Bangalore

The Department of Library and Information Science, Bangalore University, Bangalore was established in the year1974. It is offering two year integrated MLISc Course and Ph.D. in LIS. Between the years 1990 and 2010i.e. in a span of two decades, the Department has awarded 22 Ph.Ds. The following Table provides figures for the year wise award of Ph.Ds.

Table

Year	No. of Ph.Ds	Year	No. of Ph.Ds	Year	No. of Ph.Ds
1990	1	1991	-	1992	1
1993	-	1994	2	1995	1
1996	1	1997	4	1998	2
1999	1	2000	2	2001	1
2002	1	2003	1	2004	1

2005	-	2006	-	2007	1
2008	1	2009	-	2010	1
Total	**22**				

Note: The year of award of one Ph.D. was not ascertainable including the name of the Research Guide.

Among the Research Guides, Dr. A. Y. Asundi has guided (6) candidates followed by Dr. M. A. Gopinath (5), Dr. Lalita Ashwath (5), Dr. P. Sadasiva Murthy (4) and Dr. T. D. Kemparaju (2). The first scholar to obtain Ph.D. degree was Dr. T. D. Kemparaju who obtained Ph.D. Degree in the year 1990 under the guidance of Dr. M. A. Gopinath. Dr. Kempa Raju did his doctoral research on the topic "Development of Professional Skills of Library and Information Service Personal in Special Libraries".

8. DLISc, Calicut University, Calicut

The DLISc, Calicut University, Calicut introduced Ph.D. programme in 1990s. Dr. Rosamma Joseph was the first doctoral scholar to get Ph.D. in the year 1991 for her research topic entitled "A Study of Libraries, Information Needs and Use of Information Sources in Establishments in Kerala" under the guidance of Dr. M. Bavakutty. Until 2008, the Department of Library and Information Science produced 29 Ph.Ds and the year wise break up is given in the following Table.

Year	No. of Ph.Ds	Year	No. of Ph.Ds	Year	No. of Ph.Ds
1991	1	1992	1	1993	1
1994	1	1995	1	1996	-
1997	-	1998	-	1999	-
2000	-	2001	-	2002	-
2003	1	2004	4	2005	8
2006	4	2007	4	2008	3
Total	**29**				

It is evident from the above Table that no Ph.D. was awarded between the years 1996 and 2002 i.e. a span of seven years. Among the Research Supervisors, Dr. M. Bavakutty produced 11 Ph.Ds followed by Dr. Raju M. Mathew (7), Dr. V. Jalaja (6) and Dr. Rosamma Joseph (4).

9. DLIS, Gauhati University, Guwahati

DLISc, Gauhati University produced 34 Ph.Ds in Library and Information Science until May, 2013 and beginning with the year 1998. Sri Narendra Lahkar was the first Ph.D. Scholar to obtain Ph.D. degree in Library & Information Science in the year 1998 under the Supervision of Prof. A. Buragohain and who pursued doctoral research on the topic "Prospects of Automated Catalogue in three University Libraries in the Assam". There are 35 Ph.D. Scholars who have registered for Ph.D. under different supervisors or submitted their dissertations until May 2013 and waiting for the result. The following Table provides figures for year wise award of Ph.D. from the year 1998 to May 2013.

Table

Year	No. of Ph.Ds	Year	No. of Ph.Ds	Year	No. of Ph.Ds
1998	1	1999	-	2000	-
2001	-	2002	-	2003	2
2004	2	2005	1	2006	3
2007	3	2008	4	2009	6
2010	3	2011	4	2012	3
2013	2				
Total	**34**				

10. DLISc Gulbarga University, Gulbarga

The Department of Library and Information Science, Gulbarga University, Gulbarga was established in the year 1980. Presently it is offering 2 year integrated MLISc Course besides M.Phil and Ph.D. programmes.

During the years 1982 and 2013 (up to January) the Department has produced 37 Ph.Ds in Library and Information Science. The first doctoral research scholar to receive Ph.D. Degree in 1982 was Sri A. Y. Asundi under the guidance of Dr. S. R. Gunjal who happened to be the founder of the Department and who introduced Ph.D. programme. Dr. Asundi did his Doctoral Research on the topic "Development of an Unified Scheme of Common Subdivision in General Schemes of Classification." Dr. S. R. Gunjal guided successfully sixteen research scholars followed by Dr. S. L. Sangam (3), P.G. Tadsad (3) and. B. Patil (2), Dr. Lalita K. Sami (2), Dr. V. T. Kamble (3) (and Dr. B. S. Maheswarappa (3). The following Table provides figures as to the award of number of Ph.Ds in each year.

Table

Year	No. of Ph.Ds	Year	No. of Ph.Ds	Year	No. of Ph.Ds
1982	1	1983	1	1984	1
1985	1	1986	-	1987	1
1988	2	1989	1	1990	4
1991	1	1992	3	1993	1
1994	1	1995	1	1996	-
1997	-	1998	-	1999	-
2000	-	2001	-	2002	-
2003	-	2004	3	2005	1
2006	1	2007	-	2008	3
2009	-	2010	3	2011	3
2012	3				
2013 (Upto Jan. 1013)	1				
Total	**37**				

No Ph.D. was awarded from the years 1996 to 2003.

11. DLISc, Guru Nanak Dev University, Amritsar

DLISc, Guru Nanak Dev University introduced Ph.D. programme in LIS in 1990s. The first Research Scholar to get Ph.D. in LIS from the Department was Dr. M. P. Satija, who got in the year 1990. His topic for Doctoral Research was "An Investigation in to the Research Methodology of S. R. Ranganathan and his style of Writing". Dr. Satija pursued his doctoral research work under the guidance of Prof. K. Navlani. The Department has produced 28 Ph.Ds until September 2013. The year wise breakup is given in the following Table.

Table

Year	No. of Ph.Ds	Year	No. of Ph.Ds	Year	No. of Ph.Ds
1990	2	1991	-	1992	-
1993	1	1994	-	1995	2
1996	1	1997	1	1998	-
1999	1	2000	-	2001	1
2002	-	2003	-	2004	1
2005	2	2006	1	2007	4
2008	4	2009	3	2010	1
2011	1	2012	1		
2013*Until Sept. 2013	1				
Total	**28**				

Among the Research Guides Dr. Sewa Singh produced 10 Ph.Ds followed by Dr. M.P. Satija (7), Dr. Amitpal Kaur (4), Dr. H. S. Chopra (3), Dr. Navjot Kaur (3) and Prof. K. Navlani (1) the senior most Research Supervisor among the listed Supervisors.

12. DLISc, Hemachandracharya North Gujarat University, Patan

The Department of Library and Information Science, Hemachandracharya North Gujarat University, Patan awarded first Ph.D in LIS to doctoral research scholar Mr. Yogesh Kumar Patel in the year 2002 under the supervision of Dr. Sivadhanbhai Charan, for his topic on "University Library Management" and thesis was presented in Gujarati. During the years 2002 and 2012, the university has awarded 19 Ph.Ds on various facets of LIS. The year wise breakup is given in the following Table:

Table

Year	No. of Ph.Ds	Year	No. of Ph.Ds	Year	No. of Ph.Ds
2002	5	2003	2	2004	1
2005	-	2006	1	2007	-
2008	1	2009	-	2010	3
2011	1	2012	5	2013	*
Total	**19**				

**Information not available*

Among the Research Guides, Dr. Sivadhanbhai Charan has produced 9 Ph.Ds followed by Dr. M. K. Prajapati (5), Dr. C. N. Rawal (2), Dr. Gitaben Patel (2), and V. A.Thaker (1). Some of the doctoral theses were presented in Gujarati language.

13. DLISc, Jiwaji University, Gwalior

The Department of Library and Information Science, Jiwaji University, Gwalior introduced BLISc during the academic year 1984-85 followed by MLISc in 1985-86 and Ph.D. also during 1985-86. It also introduced M.Phil Programme during 2006-2007 and could conduct only two sessions which ended in 2007-

2008. Prof. S. M. Tripathi was responsible for introducing MLISc and Ph.D. programme in LIS during the academic year 1985-86 as stated already. As for the information available in the List of Ph.D. theses provided by the Department, the first Ph.D. was awarded in the year 1991 to Mohd. Burrehanuddin for his research topic titled "Indian Contribution to American Study: An investigation in to the growth of literature using bibliometrics, citation analysis" and guided by Prof. S. M.Tripathi. Even before 1991, the Department has awarded Ph.D. degrees to some research scholars. But information is not available.

Between the years 1991 and December 2013, the Department has awarded 93 Ph.D. degrees to research scholars. This figure appears to be one of the largest number of Ph.D. degrees awarded by any Indian Library School. The year wise breakup is given in the following Table.

Table

Year	No. of Ph.Ds	Year	No. of Ph.Ds	Year	No. of Ph.Ds
1991	2	1992	2	1993	5
1994	6	1995	3	1996	3
1997	6	1998	2	1999	1
2000	2	2001	6	2002	4
2003	3	2004	2	2005	2
2006	3	2007	1	2008	12
2009	13	2010	4	2011	3
2012	3				
2013 Up to Dec. 2013	5				
Total	93				

In the year 2009, 13 Ph.Ds were awarded followed by 2008 (12), 1994 (6), 2001 (6), 1993 (5) and 2013 (5). Among the Research Supervisors, Prof. J. N. Gautam produced 20 Ph.Ds followed by Prof. Hemant Kumar Sharma (20), Prof. S. M. Tripathi (5), Prof. S. S. Senghar (2), Dr. Shailini Rewadikar (2), Dr. Arvind K. Sharma (2), Dr. R. Garg (2), and Dr. A. K. Verma, Dr. K. G. Tyagi, Dr. Shialandra Kumar and M. Neeraja Setna produced one each.

Another distinct feature of this Department was engaging Joint Supervisors for guiding doctoral research scholars. There were 18 Joint Supervisors who produced thirty six (36) Ph.Ds in LIS. These Joint Supervisors include: 1. Dr. S. M. Tripathi and Prof. Krishan Kumar (1), 2. Dr. S. M. Tripathi and Dr. Nural Hassan Khan (2), 3. Prof. C. P. Vashisht and Dr. J. N. Gautam (1), 4. Prof. H. S. Senghar and Dr. J. N. Gautam (3), 5. Dr. S. M. Tripathi and Dr. R. Satyanarayana (1), 6. Dr. S. M. Tripathi and J. L. Saradana (1), 7. Dr. Nural Hassan Khan and Dr. J. N. Gautam (1), 8. Dr. S. M. Tripathi and J. K. Khanna (1), 9. Dr. S. M. Tripathi and Dr. S. R. Gupta (1), 10. Dr. S. M. Tripathi and Y. P. Dubey (1), 11. Dr. J. N. Gautam and Dr. T. A. V. Murthy (2), 12. Dr. J. N. Gautam and Prof. C. P. Vashisth (2), 13. Dr. R. G. Prasher and Dr. J. N. Gautam (1), 14. Dr. Hemant Sharma and Dr. B. K. Sharma (10), 15. Dr. Rochana Srivatsava and Dr. J. N. Gautam (2), 16. Dr. J. N. Gautam and Dr. B. K. Sharma (1), 17. Dr. J. N. Gautam and Prof. J. L. Sardana (1) and 18. Dr. J. N. Gautam and Dr. S. P. Singh (1). Among the joint research supervisors, Dr. Hemant Sharma and Dr. B. K. Sharma combination produced 10 Ph.D. holders.

14. DLISc, Karnatak University Dharwad

The Department of Library and Information Science, Karnatak University, Dharwad strait away introduced Ph.D. programme during the academic year 1974-75, without introducing M.Phil programme. The

Dept. of Library & Information Science is one of the leading Departments in the country which has produced one of the largest number of Ph.Ds in the Country. By the end of 2012, the Department has produced 82 (Up to January 2013) Ph.Ds. The following Table provides year wise breakup of figures for the number of Ph.Ds awarded between the years 1982 and 2013 up to January 2013. Prof. M. R. Kumbhar was the chief mentor of the Department and under his dynamic leadership Ph.D. programme was introduced for the first time in the entire Karnataka State or for that matter entire South India. Sri G. Bhattacharya was the first Doctoral Research Scholar to obtain Ph.D. degree in the year 1981 followed by Sri M. A. Gopinath who obtained Ph.D. Degree in the year 1982. Both did their doctoral research under the guidance of Prof. M.R.Kumbhar. Dr. Bhatta Charya pursued his doctoral research on the topic "General Theory of Subject Indexing Language".

Prof. C. R. Karisiddappa has the distinction of guiding 26 doctoral research scholars followed by Prof. S. L. Sangam (17), Prof. M. R. Kumhar (10), Prof. S. R. Ijari (8), Prof. B. D. Kumbhar (8) and Prof. K.S. Dashpandey (7). The Table provides figures for year wise award of Ph.D. Degrees between the years 1981 and 2013 (Until January 2013).

Table

Year	No. of Ph.Ds	Year	No. of Ph.Ds	Year	No. of Ph.Ds
1980	1	1981	1	1982	2
1983	4	1984	3	1985	4
1986	-	1987	2	1988	2
1989	1	1990	2	1991	2
1992	4	1993	5	1994	4
1995	3	1996	1	1997	1

1998	-	1999	5	2000	1
2001	-	2002	6	2003	3
2004	3	2005	5	2006	1
2007	4	2008	2	2009	2
2010	1	2011	3	2012	3
2013 Up to January 2013	1				
Total	**82**				

The Year 2002 saw the award of 6 Ph.Ds followed by 5 each in 1993, 1999 and 2005, 4 each in 1983, 1985, 1992 and 2007.

15. DLISc, Kuvempu University, Sankargatta, Karnataka

The Department of Library and Information Science, Kuvempu University, Shankargatta was established in the year 1993. Presently it is offering 2 year integrated MLISc Courses and research Courses leading to the award of M.Phil and Ph.D. degrees. Between the years 1997 and 2011, the Department awarded 14 Ph.D. degrees. The following Table provides figures for the 14 yearwise award of Ph.D. degrees

Table

Year	No. of Ph.Ds	Year	No. of Ph.Ds	Year	No. of Ph.Ds
1997	1	1998	-	1999	-
2000	-	2001	-	2002	-
2003	1	2004	-	2005	1
2006	-	2007	-	2008	4
2009	4	2010	-	2011	3
Total	**14**				

This is a new University compared to other Universities in Karnataka State. Among the Research Guides Dr. B. S. Biradar guided (7) Ph.D. Scholars followed by Dr. B. V. Kannappanavar (4), Dr. M. D.

Bankapur (2) and Dr. K. C. Ramakrishna Gowda (1). Dr. K. Divyananda was the first Ph.D. Research Scholar to obtain Ph.D. in the year 1997 under the guidance of Dr. M. D. Bankapur.

16. DLISc, M. S. University, Baroda

The Dept. of Library & Information Science, M. S. University, Baroda was the late comer in introducing research programme in LIS. The first Ph.D. degree in LIS was awarded in 2006 to Sangamitra Pradhan under the supervision of Prof. Kautilya Shukla. Dr.Pradhan pursued her research on the topic "Motivation and Performance Level of Library Personnel in University Libraries". Until 2011 the Department has produced only five Ph.Ds in LIS and the year wise award is presented in the following Table.

Table

Year	No. of Ph.Ds	Year	No. of Ph.Ds	Year	No. of Ph.Ds
2006	1	2007	1	2008	-
2009	-	2010	-	2011	3
2012	-	2013	-		
Total:	**5**				

Prof. Shyama Rajaram produced 3 Ph.Ds followed by Prof. Kautilya Shukla (2). Information is not available after the year 2011.

17. DLISc, Mangalore University, Mangalore

The Dept. of Library & Information Science, Mangalore University, Mangalore was established in the year 1982. It is offering 2 Year Integrated MLISc Course and Ph.D. programme. Between the year 1994 and 2011, the Department has awarded 20 Ph.Ds in LIS. Dr. D. Sivalingiah was the first research scholar to get Ph.D. in 1994 under the Supervision of Prof. V.

G. Talwar. He pursued his research on the topic "Library Facilities in Colleges in Karnataka: A Study".

The following Table provides Year wise figures on the award of Ph.Ds. Among the Research Guides Prof. A. K. Bardol guided 8 Research Scholars followed by Prof. V. G. Talwar (3), Dr. M. K. Bhandi (3), Dr. Shiva lingaiah (3) and Dr. V. M. Mahesh (3).

Table

Year	No. of Ph.Ds	Year	No. of Ph.Ds	Year	No. of Ph.Ds
1994	1	1995	-	1996	1
1997	1	1998	2	1999	-
2000	-	2001	1	2002	-
2003	2	2004	1	2005	-
2006	2	2007	4	2008	2
2009	1	2010	1	2011	1
Total	**20**				

18. DLISc, Manipur University, Manipur

The Department of Library and information Science, Manipur University, Manipur started Ph.D. programme rather late 1990s, when Prof. M. R. Kumbhar joined the Department and developed research programmes. The first Ph.D. was produced in the year 1991 under his supervision and the research scholar being Thounaojam Khomdon Singh who pursued his research on the topic "Public Library System in Manipur and how to develop it by Library Legislation". Until 2008, the Department had produced 13 Ph.Ds and the year wise break up is given in the following Table. Among the Research Supervisors, Dr. Ramansu Lahiri produced 6 Ph.Ds followed by Prof. M. R. Kumbhar (3), Dr. Th. Purnima Devi (2) and Dr.Th. Madhuri Devi (2).

Table

Year	No. of Ph.Ds	Year	No. of Ph.Ds	Year	No. of Ph.Ds
1991	1	1992	1	1993	-
1994	1	1995	-	1996	3
1997	-	1998	-	1999	1
2000	-	2001	-	2002	-
2003	-	2004	1	2005	-
2006	1	2007	1	2008	3
Total:	**13**				

19. DLISc, North Eastern Hill University (NEHU), Shillong

The Dept. of Library & Information Science, NEHU introduced Ph.D. programme in LIS in 1990s. Prof. J. C. Binwal was the main spirit behind in introducing Ph.D. programme in LIS at NEHU. Until the end of 2012, the Department has produced 20 Ph.Ds. Perhaps Dr. L. P. Pathak was the first Scholar to receive Ph.D. in 1994 in LIS under the guidance of Prof. J. C. Binwal. He pursued his doctoral research on the topic "Sociological Concept and their representation in Information Retrieval Tools". The year wise breakup of the 20 Ph.D is given in the following Table:

Table

Year	No. of Ph.Ds	Year	No. of Ph.Ds	Year	No. of Ph.Ds
1994	1	1995	1	1996	1
1997	-	1998	-	1999	1
2000	-	2001	1	2002	1
2003	5	2004	1	2005	-
2006	1	2007	3	2008	2
2009	-	2010	-	2011	1
2012	1				
Total:	**20**				

Among the Research Supervisors, Prof.J. C. Binwal produced six Ph.Ds followed by Prof.Veena Saraf (5), Prof. A. S. Chandel (3), and Prof. Moses M. Naga (1). Five theses were produced under Joint Supervision. They include Prof.Vina Saraf and Dr. N. M. Panda (1), Dr. P. Hangsing and Prof. A. S. Chandel (3) and Prof. Moses M. Naga and Dr. P. Hangsing (1). In North East India, DLISc, NEHU is one of the leading Departments to encourage research in LIS.

20. DLISc, Osmania University, Hyderabad

The Department of Library and Information Science, Osmania University, Hyderabad introduced Ph.D. programme in the year 1989, due to untiring efforts of Prof. A.A.N. Raju, to promote research and to provide an opportunity for the young faculty members of the Department to pursue research in their chosen fields. Later M.Phil programme was introduced during the academic year 1993-1994. Sri Laxman Rao was the first research scholar to obtain Ph.D. degree in 1993 from the Department. His doctoral research was on the topic "Planning and Implementation of Automated Circulation System for O.U. Library System", under the guidance of Prof. A.V. Satyanarayana Rao of the Dept. of Public Administration, Osmania University. Prof. A. A. N. Raju was the first recognized Research Supervisor in the Dept. of Library and Information Science. Sri. N. Ch. Varadaraju was the first M.Phil Research Scholar to obtain M.Phil degree and who pursued research on "Preservation of Library Materials in University Libraries: A Case study of Osmania University" under the guidance of Prof. V. Vishwa Mohan.

Between the years 1993 and 2012, the Department has produced 29 Ph.Ds and 9 M.Phils

Table

Year	No. of Ph.Ds	Year	No. of Ph.Ds	Year	No. of Ph.Ds
1993	1	1994	-	1995	2
1996	-	1997	1	1998	1
1999	4	2000	-	2001	-
2002	1	2003	2	2004	1
2005	2	2006	2	2007	1
2008	2	2009	2	2010	1
2011	3	2012	3		
Total:	**29**				

Among the Research Supervisors Prof. V. Vishwa Mohan guided (7) Ph.D. Scholars followed by Prof. A. A. N. Raju (6), Prof. S. Sudarshan Rao (6), Dr. D. B. Eshwar Reddy (3) Prof. V. Chandra Sekhar Rao (3) Prof. J.Yadagiri Reddy (2) Prof. R.V. Satyanarayana Rao (1) and Prof. N. Laxman Rao (1). The Department's progress with respect to Doctoral Research is not impressive when compared with other sister LIS Departments in the State of Andhra Pradesh.

21. DLISc, Panjab University, Chandigarh

The Dept. of Library and Information Science, Panjab University, Chandigarh was one of the oldest LIS Departments in the country. The Department introduced Ph.D. programme in LIS in 1970s and the first Ph.D. came out in the year 1976. Pandey S. K. Sharma was the first Doctoral Research Scholar to get Ph.D. in 1976 under the very able supervision of Dr. J. S. Sharma. His topic for doctoral research was "Expansion and Modification of Dewey Decimal Classification (DDC) 18th Edition for Classifying Indological Books with Special Reference to Indian Philosophy and Religion". Between the year 1976 and 2003 (Until July), the Department has produced 52

Ph.Ds and the following Table provides year wise break up of Ph.D. Degrees.

Table

Year	No. of Ph.Ds	Year	No. of Ph.Ds	Year	No. of Ph.Ds
1976	1	1977	-	1978	1
1979	-	1980	-	1981	-
1982	1	1983	-	1984	3
1985	5	1986	-	1987	1
1988	-	1989	2	1990	-
1991	1	1992	2	1993	1
1994	2	1995	-	1996	1
1997	1	1998	-	1999	-
2000	1	2001	2	2002	4
2003	3	2004	-	2005	2
2006	2	2007	3	2008	4
2009	1	2010	2	2011	3
2012	2				
2013 Until July	1				
Total	**52**				

Among the Research Supervisors, Prof. H. R. Chopra produced 12 Ph.Ds followed by Prof.Ranjana Vohra (11), Dr. J. S. Sharma (10), Dr. G. C. Bansal (4), Prof. Preeti Mahajan (4), Dr. V. K. Tikku (3), Dr. Promila (2), Dr. Preeti Goel (2), Dr. V. A. Kamath (1), Dr.(Mrs) A. K.Anand and Dr. S. L.Sharma, joint supervisors (1) and Dr. S. S. Pal (1).

22. DLISc, Panjabi University, Patiala

The DLISc, Panjabi University, Patiala introduced Ph.D. programme in LIS in the 1990s. The first Research Scholar to obtain Ph.D. in 1994 was Dr. Trisanjit Kaur who pursued her doctoral research on "Development and Growth of University Libraries and their Services in Panjab" under the Supervision of Prof. K. Navlani. Between the years 1994 and 2012, the Department has produced 15 P.Ds in LIS. The following Table provides year wise break up.

Table

Year	No. of Ph.Ds	Year	No. of Ph.Ds	Year	No. of Ph.Ds
1994	1	1995	-	1996	-
1997	1	1998	1	1999	1
2000	-	2001	-	2002	2
2003	-	2004	-	2005	2
2006	-	2007	3	2008	-
2009	1	2010	1	2011	-
2012	2				
Total	**15**				

Among Research Gujides, Prof. Jagtar Singh produced 8 Ph.Ds followed by Prof. K. Navlani (4), Dr. Trisanjit Kaur (2) andDr. S. P. Narang (1).

23. DLIS, Rashtrasant Tukadoji Maharaj Nagpur University, Nagpur

The Department of Library and Information Science, RTM Nagpur University was established in the year 1956. Initially the Dip.Lib.Sc., was started in 1956 and later BLISc, MLISc was introduced in the year 1984. A two-year integrated MLIS Course was introduced in the year 2003, dropping yearly BLISc and MLISc Courses. Doctoral programme was introduced in the year 1987. The Department until 2012, produced 53 Ph.Ds and the first Doctoral Research Scholar who obtained Ph.D. in the 1992 under the guidance of Dr. P. S. G. Kumar was Ms. D. Rajya Lakshmi who did on the topic "Impact of Ranganathan on AACR-2". Perhaps this Department produced largest number of Ph.Ds than any other

Department of Library and Information Science in Maharashtra State. Dr.P. S. G. Kumar was the main spirit behind this phenomenon. Among the Research Guides, Dr. P.S.G. Kumar guided (23) research scholars followed by Dr. D. Rajyalakshmi (9), Dr. D. R. Deshpandey (5) and Dr. M.A. Hirwade (3). The following Table provides figures for year wise award of Ph.Ds between the years 1992 and 2012 i.e. a span of two decades.

Table

Year	No. of Ph.Ds	Year	No. of Ph.Ds	Year	No. of Ph.Ds
1992	1	1993	-	1994	2
1995	-	1996	-	1997	2
1998	2	1999	1	2000	-
2001	-	2002	1	2003	1
2004	9	2005	-	2006	3
2007	2	2008	5	2009	4
2010	4	2011	10		
2012Upto Sept.2012	6				
Total	**53**				

The Year 2011 witnessed award of largest number of Ph.Ds i.e. 10 followed by 9 in 2004 and 6 in 2012.

24. DLISc, SNDT Women's University, Mumbai

The DLISc, SNDT Women's University, Mumbai, introduced Ph.D. programme in LIS in 1990s and the first Ph.D. was produced in 1996. The Research Scholar who obtained first Ph.D. in LIS was Perin Marolia who did her Doctoral Research on the topic "Expertise and qualities required for Special Librarianship" under the guidance of Dr. V. A. Kamath. During the years 1996 and 2013 (until August), the Department has produced only 10 Ph.Ds. The following Table provides year wise break up of figures.

Table

Year	No. of Ph.Ds	Year	No. of Ph.Ds	Year	No. of Ph.Ds
1996	1	1997	-	1998	-
1999	-	2000	-	2001	-
2002	1	2003	1	2004	1
2005	-	2006	-	2007	-
2008	4	2009	-	2010	1
2011	-	2012	-	2013	1
Total	**10**				

Among the Research Guides Prof. Harsha Parekh produced 6 Ph.Ds followed by Prof. Bharati Sen (2), Dr. V.A. Kamathj (1) and Dr. S. R. Ganpule (1). The Department has reputation of offering quality LIS education and turning out well educated and trained manpower. But in respect of research in LIS, it is not encouraging as shown in the above Table.

25. DLISc, Sambalpur University, Burla (Sambalpur)

The DLISc, Sambalpur University, Burla, introduced Ph.D. programme in LIS in 1990s. The first research scholar to obtain Ph.D. degree in 1993 was Shaik Allauddin who pursued his doctoral research on the topic "Libraries and Librarianship during Muslim Rule in India" under the guidance of Prof. R. K.Rout. The Department until 2012 produced 29 Ph.Ds in LIS. The following Table provides year wise breakup of figures.

Table

Year	No. of Ph.Ds	Year	No. of Ph.Ds	Year	No. of Ph.Ds
1993	1	1994	-	1995	1
1996	-	1997	2	1998	-
1999	-	2000	-	2001	2
2002	4	2003	1	2004	2
2005	2	2006	-	2007	1

2008	1	2009	-	2010	5
2011	2	2013	5		
Total:	**29**				

Among the Research Guides Dr. K. C. Panda produced 15 Ph.Ds followed by Dr. B. K. Choudhury (7), Prof. R. K. Rout (6) and Dr. K. C. Sahoo (1). It is one of the leading Departments in the State of Odhisa to promote LIS education and research.

26. DLISc, Sant Gadge Baba Amaravati University, Amravati

The Dept. of Library and Information Science, Sant Gadge Baba Amravati University was established in the year 1990. Presently the Department is offering BLISc, and MLISc Courses each of one year duration. The Department has awarded 11 Ph.Ds until 2008. The first Research Scholar to receive Ph.D. was Dr.P. M. Gajway in the year 2001. Eleven Research Scholars were pursuing research for Ph.D. degrees. The following Table provides year wise break up of Ph.Ds awarded since 2001.

Table

Year	No. of Ph.Ds	Year	No. of Ph.Ds	Year	No. of Ph.Ds
2001	2	2002	1	2003	1
2004	1	2005	-	2006	-
2007	3	2008	3		
Total	**11**				

Dr. P.M. Gajway pursued his Doctoral Research on the topic "History of Public Library Movement in Vidarbha Region of Maharashtra w.e.f. 1950-1970".

27. DLIS, Shivaji University, Kolhapur

The DLISc, Shivaji University, Kolhapur produced only 6 Ph.Ds in LISc between the years 1999 and 2007.

The first Ph.D. Scholar to get Ph.D. in LIS in 1999 was Dr. Abbas Khan who pursued his Doctoral Programme on the tgopic "Citation Analysis of Doctoral Dissertations submitted to Shivaji University, Kolhapur in Pure Sciences (1962-1992)" under the Supervision of Dr. S. R. Gunjal. The year wise breakup is given in the following Table.

Table

Year	No. of Ph.Ds	Year	No. of Ph.Ds	Year	No. of Ph.Ds
1999	1	2000	-	2001	-
2002	-	2003	-	2004	-
2005	-	2006	-	2007	5
Total	**6**				

After 2007, information about the award of Ph.Ds in LIS is not readily available. No Ph.D was awarded between the years 2000 and 2006. Among the Research Guides Prof. C. R. Karisiddappa produced 2 Ph.Ds followed by Prof. S.R. Gunjal (2) and Dr. P. V. Konnur (2). Prof. Karisiddappa, Prof. Gunjal and Prof. P. V. Konnur were all external supervisors as the LIS Department had no internal supervisors.

28. DLISc, Sri Krishna Devaraya University, Anantapur

The Department of Library and Information Science, Sri Krishna Devaraya University, Anantapur introduced M.Phil programme during the academic year 1990-91 and Ph.D. during the academic year 1991-92. So far the Department has produced 19 M.Phils and 18 Ph.Ds. Prof. P. Kamaiah was mainly responsible for introducing these two research courses against all odds.

Between the years 1999 and 2013 (up to July) the Department has produced 18 Ph.Ds. P. Rajaratnam

Chetty was the first research scholar to obtain Ph.D. in the year 1999 under the Supervision of Prof. P. Kamaiah. His topic for Doctoral Research was "Quality of Work life in the University Libraries in Andhra Pradesh". The following Table provides year wise breakup of Ph.Ds.

Table

Year	No. of Ph.Ds	Year	No. of Ph.Ds	Year	No. of Ph.Ds
1999	1	2000	-	2001	-
2002	-	2003	1	2004	1
2005	3	2006	2	2007	2
2008	3	2009	1	2010	1
2011	-	2012	1		
2013 Until July 2013	2				
Total	**18**				

Among the Research Supervisors, Prof. P. Kamaiah produced 9 Ph.Ds followed by Dr. P. Rajaratnam Chetty (5), Dr. Ravinder (3) and Dr. P. Pratap Reddy (1).

29. DLISc, Sri Venkateshwara University, Tirupati

The DLISc, Sri Venkateshwara University, Tirupati produced first Ph.D. in 1990 in T. Rajagopal, supervised by Prof. G. V . S. L. Narasimha Raju. Dr. Rajagopal pursued his Doctoral Research on the topic "A Critical Study of Information seeking behavior of Medical Specialists in Madras City".

Table

Year	No. of Ph.Ds	Year	No. of Ph.Ds	Year	No. of Ph.Ds
1990	1	1991	-	1992	1
1993	1	1994	-	1995	2
1996	-	1997	2	1998	2
1999	2	2000	3	2001	1

2002	-	2003	3	2004	1
2005	-	2006	-	2007	2
2008	2	2009	4	2010	2
2011	9	2012	5		
Total	**43**				

Among the Research Supervisors, Prof. V. Pulla Reddy produced 10 Ph.Ds followed by Prof K. Padmini (8), Prof. D. Chandran (7), Prof. N. Guruswamy Naidu (6) and Prof. T. Rajagopal (5). Three Research Scholars submitted their Ph.D. dissertations under the Supervision of Prof. D. Chandran in the year 2013 and the result is awaited.

30. Thakur Ranmath Singh Autonomous College, Rewa

This College is affiliated to Awadesh Pratap Singh University, Rewa. Kumari Sheela Goel was the first Ph.D. Scholar to get P.h.D. in the year 2001. She pursued her Doctoral Research on the topic "College Libraries in M.P: An Evaluation" under the guidance of Prof. N. R. Satyanarayana of DLISc, Lucknow University who acted as External Supervisor. So far this College has produced 19 Ph.Ds and most of them were in Hindi. The year wise breakup is given the following Table.

Table

Year	No. of Ph.Ds	Year	No. of Ph.Ds	Year	No. of Ph.Ds
2001	2	2002	-	2003	-
2004	-	2005	1	2006	-
2007	1	2008	2	2009	2
2010	4	2011	2	2012	5
Total	**19**				

The year 2012 saw the award of largest number of Ph.Ds. Among the Research Supervisors Dr. R. K.

Sharma produced 10 Ph.Ds followed by Prof. N. R. Satyanarayana (8) and Dr. A. K. Verma (1).

31. DLISc, The University of Burdwan, Burdwan (West Bengal)

The DLISc, the University of Burdwan is one of leading Departments in LIS in West Bengal. The Department has produced 28 Ph.Ds in LIS until May 2013. Manoranjan Mahapatgra was the first Doctoral Research Scholar who was awarded Ph.D. in the year 1984 under the Supervision of Sri Bijoynath Mukherjee. Dr. Mahapatra pursued his doctoral research on the topic "Growth of Literature and Citation Pattern among the Indian Journals in the field of Botany: 1950-80". Prof. P. B. Barua laid strong foundation for Doctoral Research Programme n LIS and produced 9 Ph.Ds followed by Prof. Subal Chandra Biswas (7) and Prof. Tridip Tripathi (6). The following Table provides year wise breakup of Ph.Ds awarded between the years 1984 and May 2013.

Table

Year	No. of Ph.Ds	Year	No. of Ph.Ds	Year	No. of Ph.Ds
1984	1	1985	-	1986	-
1987	-	1988	1	1989	-
1990	1	1991	1	1992	3
1993	-	1994	1	1995	2
1996	-	1997	-	1998	-
1999	-	2000	-	2001	-
2002	-	2003	1	2004	1
2005	-	2006	2	2007	1
2008	2	2009	2	2010	2
2011	-	2012	3	2013	4
Total	**28**				

32. DLISc, University of Delhi, Delhi

The DLISc, University of Delhi was established in the year 1946 and later introduced M.Phil and Ph.D. programs. It introduced Ph.D. degree in 1951 and M.Phil degree in 1976. As stated elsewhere, the first research scholar to obtain Ph.D. Degree in LIS from an Indian University was Dr. D. B. Krishna Rao who obtained Ph.D. degree in LIS in the year 1957 for his Doctoral Research on the topic "Facet Analysis and Depth Classification of Agriculture" under the privileged guidance of Dr. S. R. Ranganathan. Until the year 2011, the Department has produced 59 Ph.Ds and 116 M.Phils. Prof. K. P. Singh in her paper presented at IATLIS National Conference held at Gujarat University, Ahmedabad in 2011 traces the genesis and growth of LIS research at the Department of Library and Information Science, University of Delhi and provides the following Table indicating chronological distribution of LIS Research.

Table

Year	No. of Ph.Ds	Year	No. of Ph.Ds	Year	No. of Ph.Ds
1957	1	1958	-	1959	-
1960	-	1961	-	1962	-
1963	-	1964	-	1965	-
1966	-	1967	-	1968	-
1969	-	1970	-	1971	-
1972	-	1973	-	1974	-
1975	-	1976	-	1977	-
1978	-	1979	-	1980	-
1981	-	1982	-	1983	1
1984	-	1985	-	1986	1
1987	-	1988	2	1989	1
1990	-	1991	1	1992	3
1993	1	1994	2	1995	2
1996	1	1997	2	1998	1

1999	5	2000	3	2001	1
2002	4	2003	2	2004	3
2005	1	2006	4	2007	2
2008	2	2009	2	2010	6
2011	5				
Total	**59**				

Source: Prof. K.P.Singh. LIS Research: A Case Study of Dept. of Library and Information Science, University of Delhi, Delhi. *In LIS Education, Research and Training: Vision 2020, IATLIS 2011*. Papers of the National Conference, Ahmedabad, 26-28, November 2011. Patiala, DLISc, Panjabi University, 2011. Pp.292-312.

For almost two and half decades i.e. from 1958 to 1982 not a single Ph.D. was awarded by the Department. This was because lack of Research Guides in the Department to guide the doctoral research scholars and for any other reason.

The above figures were not impressive considering that DLISc, University of Delhi is one of the oldest Departments in the Country and Ph.D. programme was introduced way back in 1951. During five and half decades (1951-2011) it produced only 59 Ph.Ds, whereas some of the DLISc Departments which were established later produced more number of Ph.Ds.

Among the Research Supervisors, Prof. P. B. Mangla produced 9 Ph.Ds followed by Prof. J. L. Sardana (8), Dr. Shailendra Kumar (7), Prof. Krishan Kumar (6) Prof. (Mrs) S. P. Singh (5), Prof. S. R. Gupta (4), Dr. R. K. Bhatt (4), Dr.(Mrs) P. K. Walia (3), Prof. D. S. Agarwal (2), Prof. M. M. Kashyap (2) and one each by Prof. C. P. Vashisht, Prof. Kamaleshwar and Dr. M. Madhusudan. In addition 4 Ph.Ds were produced under joint supervision. These include Prof. D. S. Agarwal and Prof. C. P. Vashisht (1), Prof. S. R. Gupta and Prof. D. S. Agarwal (1), Dr. Shailender Kumar and Prof. S. R. Gupta (2).

33. DLISc, University of Jammu, Jammu

DLISc, University of Jammu introduced Ph.D. programme in 1990s and the first Ph.D. in LIS was awarded in 1994. Ms. Sangeeta Devi was the first Doctoral Research Scholar to get Ph.D. in 1994 for her topic "Human Resource Development needs as depicted by the Survey of Automation of Scientific and Technical Libraries in India" under the guidance of Prof. I. V. Malhan. Until 2012, the Department has produced only 10 Ph.Ds in LIS and the year wise breakup is given in the following Table.

Table

Year	No. of Ph.Ds	Year	No. of Ph.Ds	Year	No. of Ph.Ds
1994	1	1995	1	1996	-
1997	-	1998	1	1999	2
2000	-	2001	-	2002	-
2003	-	2004	-	2005	1
2006	-	2007	1	2008	1
2009	-	2010	1	2011	-
2012	1				
Total	**10**				

In the last two decades i.e. 1994-2012, the Department has produced only 10 Ph.Ds which was not encouraging. Among the Research Supervisors Prof. I. V. Malhan produced 7 Ph.Ds followed by Prof. Sangita Gupta (2) and 1 by Joint Research Supervisors Prof. A. N. Sidhu and Prof. I. V. Malhan.

34. DLISc, University of Kashmir, Srinagar

The DLISc, University of Kashmir, Srinagar introduced Ph.D. programme in LIS in the year 1989. Mr. W. A. Alvi was the first research scholar to be registered for Ph.D. as a supplicant followed by Mr. S. M Shafi in the year 1990. Dr. W. A. Alvi did his doctoral research on the topic "Resource Sharing among University and College Libraries in Jammu and Kashmir". Both of them got Ph.D. degrees in the year 1994. So far the Department has produced twelve Ph.Ds, the latest being Mr. Zahoor Ahmed Sofi who got his jPh.D.in the year 2011. Among the Research Supervisors, Prof. S. M. Shafi guided eight research scholars successfully followed by Prof. W. A. Alvi who guided two research scholars until 2011. The following Table provides figures for the year wise award of Ph.Ds.

Table

Year	No. of Ph.Ds	Year	No. of Ph.Ds	Year	No. of Ph.Ds
1994	2	1995	1	2007	1
2009	1	2010	1	2011	6
Total	**12**				

35. DLISc, University of Lucknow, Lucknow

The Department of Library and Information Science, University of Lucknow, Lucknow started Ph.D. programme in LIS rather late when compared with other Universities in the State and the Country. The first Scholar to obtain Ph.D. in LIS was Babita Jaiswal in the year 2000 under the supervision of Prof. N. R. Satyanarayana. She pursued her doctoral research on the topic "Pattern of Communication among Scientists in Lucknow". By the end of 2012, the Department was able to produce fourteen Ph.Ds and all under the supervision of Prof. N. R. Satyanarayana. The following Table provides year wise breakup of award of Ph.Ds.

Table

Year	No. of Ph.Ds	Year	No. of Ph.Ds	Year	No. of Ph.Ds
2000	1	2001	1	2002	1
2003	4	2004	-	2005	-
2006	1	2007	2	2008	1
2009	-	2010	1	2011	-
2012	2	2013	-		
Total	**14**				

36. DLIS, University of Madras, Chennai

DLISc, University of Madras, Chennai is one of the oldest DLIS Departments in the Country which produced very prominent library professionals such as Prof. S. Parthasarathy, Prof. A. Neelameghan, Prof. B. P. Shenoy and Prof. M. A. Gopinath to mention a few. The credit of introducing Ph.D. programme in LIS goes to Prof. P. Gangadhara Rao in 1980s. The first Scholar to get Ph.D. in LIS in the year 1989 is Dr. Manorama Raju who pursued her doctoral research on the topic "Personnel Management of University Libraries: A Study of Organizational Climate" under the guidance of Prof. P. Gangadhar Rao. Until August 2013, the Department produced 57 Ph.Ds in LIS and the year wise breakup is given in the following Table:

Table

Year	No. of Ph.Ds	Year	No. of Ph.Ds	Year	No. of Ph.Ds
1989	2	1990	-	1991	1
1992	-	1993	-	1994	1
1995	1	1996	1	1997	-
1998	2	1999	3	2000	1
2001	2	2002	4	2003	5
2004	6	2005	5	2006	5
2007	8	2008	1	2009	3
2010	1	2011	-	2012	3
2013 Until August 2013	2				
Total	**57**				

The year 2007 witnessed award of largest number of eight Ph.Ds than any other year between 1989 and 2013. Among the Research Supervisors Prof. Manorama Srinath and Prof. B. Ramesh Babu produced 16 Ph.Ds each followed by Prof. K. S. Raghavan (12), Prof. A. Amudavalli (9), Prof. P. Gangadhar Rao (2) and Dr. R. Vengan (2).

37. DLISc, University of Mysore, Mysore

The University of Mysore is one of the oldest Universities in Karnataka State. The Dept. of Library and Information Science introduced Ph.D. programme during the academic year 1975-76. The first person to obtain Ph.D. degree was K.S. Raghavan who obtained in the year 1982 and who pursued his doctoral research under the supervision of Prof. A. Neelameghan on the topic "Postulate based permuted subject indexing: A Study of its Effectiveness".

During the last 31 years i.e. between 1982 and 2012, the University awarded 60 Ph.D. Degrees. The following Table provides year wise breakup of the award of Ph.Ds.

Table

Year	No. of Ph.Ds	Year	No. of Ph.Ds	Year	No. of Ph.Ds
1982	1	1983	-	1984	1
1985	-	1986	-	1987	2
1988	1	1989	-	1990	-
1991	-	1992	2	1993	-
1994	2	1995	3	1996	-
1997	2	1998	-	1999	1
2000	-	2001	2	2002	7
2003	2	2004	2	2005	3
2006	2	2007	1	2008	7
2009	3	2010	8	2011	2
2012	6				
Total	**60**				

Among the Research Supervisors, Prof. V. G. Talwar produced the largest number of Ph.Ds i.e. 15 followed by Prof. H. A. Khan (7), Prof. N. B.Pangannaya (5), Dr. Mallinath Kumbhar (5) and Dr. Khaiser Nikam(4). In the year 2010, largest numbers of 8 Ph.Ds were awarded than any other year between 1982 and 2012.

38. DLISc, University of Pune, Pune

The Department of Library and Information Science, University of Pune, Pune was established in the year 1958 and Diploma Course in Library Science was started during the academic year 1958-59. In the year 1965 BLISc Course was started and an integrated MLISc Course (2-Years) was started in the year 2002 and in the same year M.Phil and Ph.D. programmes were also introduced. Until the year 2008, the Department has produced 43 Ph.Ds. Among the Ph.D. Supervisors, Dr. M. R. Konnur produced more Ph.Ds numbering (7), followed by Dr. J. Deshpandey (6), Dr. S. G. Mahajan (6), Dr. M. R. Rishwadkar (5) and Dr. S. R. Ganpule (4). Sri M. R. Konnur was the first doctoral research scholar to obtain first Ph.D. degree in the year 1986 under the able guidance of Dr. M. R. Rishwadkar. Dr. Konnur did doctoral research on the topic "Transnational Library Relation: The Indo-American Experience". The following Table provides year wise figures for the award of Ph.Ds between the years 1986 and 2008 i.e. a span of twenty two years.

Table

Year	No. of Ph.Ds	Year	No. of Ph.Ds	Year	No. of Ph.Ds
1986	1	1987	1	1988	-
1989	1	1990	1	1991	1
1992	2	1993	1	1994	-
1995	2	1996	-	1997	-

1998	4	1999	3	2000	1
2001	2	2002	1	2003	2
2004	2	2005	4	2006	3
2007	4	2008	7		
Total	**43**				

In the year 2008 seven Ph.Ds were awarded followed by 4 each in 1998, 2005 and 2007.

39. DLISc, Utkal University, Bhubaneshwar

DLISc, Utkal University, Bhubaneshwar introduced Ph.D. programme in LIS in later part of 1980s and the first person to receive Ph.D. degree in LIS was Dr. R. K. Baliarsingh in 1990 under the guidance of Dr. M. Mohapatra. Dr. Baliarsingh pursued his Doctoral Research on the topic "Information needs of different Communities: A Survey of Puri District of Orissa". The Department has produced 31 Ph.Ds in LIS until the end of 2012 and year wise break up is presented in the following Table.

Table

Year	No. of Ph.Ds	Year	No. of Ph.Ds	Year	No. of Ph.Ds
1990	1	1991	-	1992	3
1993	2	1994	-	1995	-
1996	1	1997	-	1998	1
1999	4	2000	2	2001	1
2002	-	2003	2	2004	1
2005	3	2006	2	2007	2
2008	1	2009	-	2010	1
2011	3	2012	1		
Total	**31**				

Among the Research Supervisors, Dr. M. Mohapatra produced 6 Ph.Ds followed by Dr. B.Parida (4), Dr. Gayatri Mohapatra (4), Prof.C. R. Karisiddappa (3), Dr. P. Padhi (3), Prof. K. Siva Reddy (2), Prof. S. R.

Gunjal (1), Dr. K. C. Panda (1), Dr. B. B. Shukla (1). Among the Research Guides, Prof. C. R. Karisiddappa, Prof. K. Siva Reddy and Prof. S. R. Gujal were the external guides as there were no sufficient guides to guide the Ph.D. Scholars in LIS in the Department.

40. DLISc, Swami Ramanand Thirth Maratwada University (SRTMU), Nanded

The Department of Library and Information Science, SRTMU was established in the year 1999 the youngest Department in the State of Maharashtra and started offering BLISc and MLISc Courses. Presently it is offering two year integrated MLISc Course and Ph.D. programme. So far the Department has guided 4 Ph.Ds and five research scholars have been pursuing doctoral research for Ph.D. Degree.

REFERENCES

1. Raju, A. A. N. LIS Education and Research in Andhra Pradesh. *In* Dynamics of Librarianship in the knowledge Society. V4. *Ed* by D. Chandran, *etal.* Delhi, B. R. Publishing Corporation, 2012. Pp.1264-1277,
2. Ibid.

9

TRAINING OF LIS PROFESSIONALS

9.1. INTRODUCTION

In the preceeding Chapters, educating the LIS professionals by the formal institutions such as Library Associations, Universities and other learned institutions has been presented. These agencies provide education to turnout library professionals at different levels such as semi-professional and professional levels. Semi-professional level includes CLISc and Professional levels include BLISc and MLISc degree holders. Beyond MLISc degree many of the Universities offer research courses leading to the award of M.Phil and Ph.D. degrees. The word 'education' is used in the sense that to educate the persons having basic qualifications as required by each course in LIS and to impart basic knowledge and practical training in a specified duration and secure a formal degree or certificate from the imparting Institution. After obtaining the formal certificates / degrees, the candidates are eligible to enter into job market for employment in Libraries / Information Centres and LIS Departments of the Universities and other such institutions in the Country and elsewhere.

The word 'training' is used in the context that to improve one's capability, capacity, performance and acquisition of new knowledge and skills in ones work place and to keep track of developments in one's own field beyond one's basic professional qualifications so as to compete with others throughout his / her professional career. There are several avenues available for LIS professionals including LIS teachers to get 'trained' themselves so as to survive in this competitive world and climb the ladder to reach top positions.

Definitions

According to Oxford English Dictionary (OED) unabridged edition, training has been defined as "discipline and instruction directed to the development of powers or formation of character; education, reading, bringing up; systematic instruction and exercise in some art, profession or occupation with a view to proficiency in it"[1]. A. S. Antai defined 'training' as "the systematic development of Employee's knowledge, skills and attitudes that are required for an organization to meet its goals"[2].

Wikipedia, explains the concept of training as "the acquisition of knowledge, skills and competencies as a result of the teaching of vocational or practical skills and knowledge that relate to specific useful competencies. Training has specific goals of improving one's capability, capacity and performance. It forms the core of apprenticeships and provides the backbone of content. People within many professions and occupations, may refer to this sort of training as professional development"[3].

Continuing Education

The word 'training' is used in broader sense which includes 'Continuing Education' and this concept has been used frequently by LIS teachers and professional in their writings. There appears to a lot of literature on continuing education for librarians, library professionals and LIS teachers. In the succeeding paras the word 'continuing education' is used in place of training. R. S. Saxena explains the concept of continuing education as "the process through which an individual updates and upgrades his or her already acquired knowledge in any particular field of specialization, profession or vocation so as to improve efficiency in one's profession"[4]. A.L.A. Guidelines state that "all activities that leads to efforts by the individuals to upgrade one's knowledge, competence in any field of specialization are continuing educational activity"[5]. Gopinath observed that "continuing education is a kind of life time learning. It is kind of self renewal of an urge for individuals to keep abreast with the chosen field of knowledge and profession"[6]. Stone defines continuing education as "all the activities and efforts by individuals to upgrade his knowledge, abilities, competencies and understanding in his field of work or specialization so that he can become more effective professional"[7].

9.2. OBJECTIVES

LIS personnel working in various capacities in various types of libraries and information centres and LIS teachers required to upgrade their knowledge and skills to put better performance in their respective work environment. Training at regular intervals helps the trainees to keep abreast of latest developments and trends in their fields of work and enable them to perform qualitatively in their day to day work environment. Experts in the field of training identified the following objectives which may equally applicable to the field of LIS.

1. To impart knowledge and skills to the trainees so as to enable them to stand in good stead to perform their duties effectively.
2. To develop the trainees to use their potential for the progress and success of their parent organization.
3. To develop individual trainee his skills vis-à-vis his present job.
4. To develop individual trainee in relation to his present as well as future job expectations and / or role.
5. To develop team work and team spirit in an organization.
6. To develop and promote enabling capabilities among the trainees so as to help and establish healthy organization.

With respect to LIS Teachers, Sardana and Krishan Kumar[8] listed the following objectives:

1. To help broaden and develop professional knowledge.
2. To keep them up to date and well informed.
3. To prepare them to meet the challenge of changing needs.
4. To learn about and implement new ideas, methods and techniques, etc.
5. To improve effectiveness of teaching, research and publication activity (in case of LIS teachers).
6. To assist personal professional growth and development, and
7. To achieve job satisfaction.

Houle[9] identified the following objectives of continuing education.

1. To keep up with new knowledge.
2. To establish mastery of new concepts on one's own profession.
3. To continue the study of the basic discipline that supports one's profession.
4. To grow as a person as well as a professional.

T. N. Rajan[10] observed that "the main objective of continuing education programme is to provide opportunities to practitioners to update their professional knowledge of current trends and practices in a particular area relevant to their requirements so that they could contribute their best. It should be open to different categories of personnel at all levels of work in an organization".

9.3. NEED FOR CONTINUING EDUCATION

Knowledge is dynamic, ever-growing and continuous. New ideas, concepts, theories and principles are being added to every subject field. Library and Information Science is no exception in this regard. Those who work in this field in various capacities need to update the professional knowledge and skills from time to time so as to offer better services to their clientele. This is equally applicable to LIS teaching community to turn out better products from the LIS Schools.

The prime aim of LIS is to provide information services and products which will help workers in other fields in pursuit of study, teaching and research in their respective areas of specialization. Conversely any deficiency in Library and Information Services to the Clientele at large may affect the development of other subject fields. Therefore there is an essential need for LIS personnel to have continuing education programmes at regular intervals so as to enable them to update their professional knowledge and skills. Guha[11] observed that "developments in some of the Sciences have been quite fast during the last few decades. This has brought additional responsibilities on the information workers. As a consequence, Information Science itself has also been changing rapidly during the last two decades or so. These changes and developments have been so rapid that at times even trained information workers have felt as if each day demanded broader perspectives so to say. It is against this background that we have to consider any plan or programme of continuing education of library and information workers".

Rewadikar[12] identified the following four factors viz:

1. Growth in Science and Technology,
2. Advances in Library and Information Techniques,
3. Inter Disciplinary nature of LIS, and
4. Manpower planning which necessitated having continuing education programmes for LIS personnel.

Gupta[13] identified the following factors which necessitated continuing education for librarians.

1. Large amount of new knowledge and its availability in various forms, and advances in Information Communication Technologies.
2. Changes in users' requirements and as a consequence and their demands on LIS services.
3. Increased pressure on Library System, which results in extra pressure on existing LIS Services.
4. Increase pressure on Library System results in changes in existing library techniques, services,

use of variety of new equipment, etc.

5. To meet the changes in the library system and its services and to adjust in the new environment, LIS personnel need continuing education programmes.

9.4. SUGGESTED AREAS FOR CEP

According to changing needs of the LIS personnel and developments in the field of LIS and especially the emergence of Information and Communication Technologies, and Internet and related developments in the fields, the areas have to be identified carefully for CEP which will go a long way in training the LIS personnel and LIS teachers. While identifying the areas for COE, the developments which have already taken place and the emerging technologies in the fields of LIS have to b e taken into consideration. T. N. Rajan[14] has identified three broad types of courses which include: 1. Refresher Courses, 2. Course on Information Systems relating to specific area, and 3. Course on Information Handling. He has further suggested the following specific subject areas for conducting CEP.

1. Information Sources and Media:
   — Patent Literature
   — Trade Literature
   — Literature on microforms
   — Machine readable forms of literature
2. Information Systems – National and International:
   — International Information Networks
   — INIS
   — INSDEC
   — NISSAT
3. Information Processing:

- — Trends in subject indexing and information retrieval
- — Condensation, consolidation and repackaging, preparation of abstracts, digests, technical briefs, reviews, trend reports, state of art - reports.

4. Information Services:
   - — User Studies
   - — Preparation of various information products and services
   - — National document supply service
5. Information Technology:
   - — Computer applications in information handling
   - — computerized databases and their utilization
   - — programming languages
   - — telecommunication technology
   - — Reprographic and micrographic technology
6. Management of Information System / Centre:
   - — Application of management technique
   - — Evaluation of information systems

The duration of these courses may be of two days and six weeks and more practice oriented. It would be better if these courses in the nature of workshops. Some of the above subject areas have lost their significance in view of the advances in Information and Communication Technologies (ICT) and their application in Library and Information Centres (LICs).

In view of the trends and developments in LIS and the advent and adaptation Information and Communication technologies in the management of Library and Information Centres (LICs) at the beginning of 21st century, the need for more continuing education programme has been felt by the profession. Experienced LIS teachers have suggested the following areas for CEP programmes. These include:

1. Database and Internet search strategies
2. KML and SGML
3. Designing digital libraries and institutions repositories
4. Creation of blogs and blogging
5. Web design and updation
6. Migration from AACR & MARC to RDA
7. Integration of proprietary resources with open access resources in LICs
8. Electronic Resources Management (ERM) software systems
9. E-learning / online learning packages
10. Taxonomics and outologies
11. Packaging and repacking information
12. Change management
13. Knowledge management
14. Data Warehousing
15. Library 2.0
16. Intellectual Property Rights
17. Data Mining
18. Concept Mapping
19. D-space
20. E-Prints and
21. Information Brokering[15]

This list is only suggestive.

Rudra Rajan[16] has suggested the following areas for CEP:

1. Creation of databases
2. MARC-21
3. Web 2.0 tools
4. Electronic newspaper clipping services
5. Content management software
6. Development in digital library, institutional repositories and IPR issues
7. Creation of information microforms, CD-ROM, DVD etc.
8. Designing of interfaces of Online reference services
9. Networking of libraries and E-consortia, and
10. Handling of library management software, e-books, e-journals

Those who wish to conduct CEP in LIS must have the required expertise, infrastructure facilities and manpower so as to do justice to such CEP. However, of late, the intensity of such programmes has not been felt by the profession.

9.5. AGENCIES ORGANIZING CONTINUING EDUCATION PROGRAMMES

There are several agencies which offer continuing education programmes for LIS professionals and LIS teachers. These include: 1. LIS Schools of Indian Universities, 2. Professional Associations at State and National levels, 3. National Organizations, and 4. International Organizations.

1. LIS Schools of Indian Universities

There are nearly hundred LIS Schools of the Indian Universities in the Country, which offer formal education programmes such as: BLIS, MLIS, MLISc (2-years), M.Phil and Ph.D. programmes. In addition to these formal programmes, LIS schools in the Country also offer a variety of continuing education programmes such as: National Seminars / Conferences / Workshop and practical training programmes in Cataloguing, Classification and Computer Applications in Libraries. In addition, other programmes include: The Job Trainings, Assigning Special Projects, Excursions / Visits to fully computerized LICs and Discussion Forums. Earlier UGC was supporting LIS Schools to organize National / International Conferences / Seminars on various facets of LIS. In addition to UGC other agencies such as DST, CSIR, ICAR, ICSSR, ICMR have been supporting LIS Schools to organize CEP programmes on the emerging areas of LIS. The proceedings of these Seminars / Conferences have been brought out in print form for the benefit of LIS teachers and working librarians of all categories. In addition, these publications enriched LIS literature and are very useful for prospective LIS teachers / practicing librarians.

The University of Hyderabad Library offering post-graduate Diploma in Library Automation and Networking Course (PGTD LAN) since 1998 under distance mode. The duration is for one academic year and consists of six courses: 1. Introduction to Information Technology, 2. Information Systems, 3. Bibliographic Database Management Systems, 4. Library Automation, 5. Library Networks and 6. Dissertation / Project Work. The Course is available for those possessing a minimum of BLIS degree. Separate Centre for Competency in digital libraries and e-learning Lab facility is available for PGD LAN students[17].

2. Professional Associations

National professional associations such as: 1. Indian Library Association (ILA), Delhi, 2. Indian Association of Special Libraries and Information Centres (IASLIC), Kolkata, 3. Indian Association of Teachers of Library and Information Science (IATLIS), 4. Association of Govt. Librarians and Information Specialists (AGLIS) and many more national and State level Associations have been organizing from time to time national seminars / conferences at various centres in India for the benefit of their members. Participation in these national conferences / seminars / workshops will immensely benefit the professionals to interact with the seniors in the profession, and to exchange ideas and update their knowledge in various subject fields of LIS and helps to broaden the mental horizons of participants, especially the young professionals.

The above mentioned three National Professional Associations such as: ILA, IASLIC and IATLIS organize National Seminars / Conferences at different parts of the country which enables the professionals to participate in such conferences / seminars. These National Associations bring out pre-conference volumes which include the papers to be presented at a particular Conference. These volumes are of immense help to the professionals / LIS teachers to update their knowledge on various facets of LIS.

In addition, there are many national / state level professional associations which organize national / state level conferences / seminars / workshops for the benefit of LIS professionals.

3. National Organisations

There are several independent national organizations which conduct basic training and continuing education programmes for LIS personnel. These include: INSDOC (since merged with NISCAIR in 2002), NISCAIR, DRTC, INFLIBNET, NIC and DST which have been organizing long-term and short-term training programmes for the benefit of LIS personnel. These programmes are not on traditional courses as being offered by LIS Schools in the Country, but are slanted towards documentation, information technology (IT), telecommunication developments and Internet, etc[18]. For example, DRTC, Bangalore convenes an All Indian Seminar in mid-December each year to keep up continuing research and to exchange ideas with practicing document a lists and other research workers on subjects of current interest in the field. The annual seminars are bcing conducted regularly since 1963. Again since 1969, DRTC has been conducting Refresher Seminar every year in May. This is meant for new entrants to the profession or persons who want to update their knowledge in some branch of LIS. The discussions are based on a working paper prepared by the staff members of DRTC. It also includes some practical work to be done by the participants.

Likewise INSDOC earlier used to offer short-term courses on reprography, computer applications in libraries, technical translation, and design and development of databases. During the 1960s and 1970s INSDOC offered the following short-term training and workshops. 1. Regional Training Course in Scientific Documentation (1963), 2. Workshop on Planning of Branch Information Centres in the CSIR, 3. Workshop on CHEM / SDI Search Editing and 4. Science Policy Exchange Information System (SPINES). Other Government of India Organizations such as BARC, Publications and Information Directorate (PID), Dept. of Science and Technology (DST) offer short-term

Courses from time to time for the benefit of LIS Personnel.

International Organizations

International Organizations such as: UNESCO, FID, IFLA, ISKO, ISO, WIPO and ICA offer short and long term Courses / Workshops for the benefit of LIS professionals especially for those in developing Countries. Sometimes these international organizations organize their annual international conferences / seminars in India. Attending such Conferences / Seminars by LIS professionals will go a long way in updating their professional knowledge and help meeting international experts for exchange of ideas and gaining new experiences at the international fora. If these International Conferences were held elsewhere, very few professionals from India can afford to attend them.

For example Library Schools Sections of IFLA formulates several Continuing Educational Programmes for educators of LIS. It also acts as clearing house of information for education, training and research. UNISIST programme of UNESCO also launched regional Seminars for the benefit of professionals especially in developing countries. These include short-term courses on documentation, information science and LIS education.

Refresher Courses and Orientation Programmes

The National Policy on Education (NPE) recognized the need for improving the quality of Education and Status of the teacher by providing opportunities for professional and career development[19]. It was proposed to enhance the motivation of the teachers through systematic orientation / refresher courses in specific subject fields, techniques and methodologies. For building up motivation among the teaching community the NPE proposed the following steps[20].

a) To organize specially designated Orientation Programmes in teaching methodology, educational psychology, pedagogy etc. for all new teachers.

b) To organize refresher courses for serving teachers to cover every teacher at least once in five years.

c) To encourage teachers to participate in seminars, symposia, etc.

UGC Scheme for Orientation / Refresher Courses for Academic Staff

In consonance with its VII Five Year Plan proposals with a view to implement the NPE programme of action, the UGC has formulated in the first instance, a scheme for the orientation of newly appointed college and university lecturers. The UGC also envisaged a scheme of Refresher Courses for all serving teachers in colleges and university Departments[21].

The Refresher Courses will provide opportunities for serving teachers a forum to keep abreast of all the latest advances in various subject fields. With the introduction of Orientation / Refresher Courses, the UGC fervently believes that the culture of learning and self improvement will become an integral part of the educational system[22, 23].

9.6. ACADEMIC STAFF COLLEGES (ASCS)

In the year 1987, forty seven Academic Staff Colleges (ASCs) were established in various Universities all over the Country and the number has been increasing steadily. So far there are sixty six (66) ASCs in India. These ASCs have been conducting Orientation

Programmes, Subject Refresher Courses, Interaction Programmes and Short-term Courses for the benefit of University / College teachers and research scholars. So far a few hundred thousand academic administrators, staff members and research scholars have been trained through these training courses all over the Country[24].

Subject Refresher Courses

For LIS Teachers / Librarians not below the rank of Lecturer / Asst. Librarian, with fair length of service, the UGC has introduced a scheme of Subject Refresher Courses. This Course is aimed at improving the subject comprehension of Lecturers / Librarians, having more than eight years of service are eligible for this Course. The accent is exclusively on updating the subject knowledge of the participants. The UGC has stipulated that senior most staff member of the Department in the subject field concerned be nominated as Course Coordinator. The Course Coordinator is responsible for identifying thrust areas in the field of Library and Information Science and draws a detailed syllabus. The Coordinator is also expected to prepare schedule of sessions, identifying resource persons, monitor the progress of the course academically[25].

Objectives of Subject Refresher Courses in LIS

Prof. N. B. Pangannaya and Prof. V. G. Talwar have identified the following objectives:

1. To update the knowledge of working librarians and teachers in LIS in various branches in the field of LIS.
2. To equip them with the latest information in different areas of LIS.
3. To discuss various problems that the LIS teachers

and professionals encounter in class room teaching and library organization and management respectively and find out suitable solutions to them.

4. To discuss the contents of core syllabus of LIS courses of various Universities and suggest necessary modifications if required, and
5. To equip teachers and librarians with required skills so as to make teachers to impart better education to their students and to prepare librarians to serve their users better[26].

Academic Staff College (ASC), Osmania University (OU)

The first Refresher Course (RC) was conducted by the ASC-OU from 1 – 26, August 1989. Forty professionals working in College / University Libraries were selected from the catchment area as per UGC guidelines. Persons holding senior positions in Academic Libraries and also Faculty Members of the Department of Library and Information Science, O.U. served as Resources Persons. In addition to lectures and demonstrations, a field trip was arranged to visit ICRISAT Library for practical observation of Library Automation[27].

Course Contents

Keeping in view the trends and developments in Academic Librarianship and the requirements of professionals working in College / University Libraries and teachers working in LIS Schools, a Course was designed to be conducted by ASC – OU. Broadly the Course Contents were:

1. Academic Librarianship – Concept, aims and objectives

2. Policy Perspectives
3. Issues in Management
4. Collection Development
5. Physical and Bibliographical Control
6. Academic Library Services
7. Resource sharing and Networking
8. Library Building and Equipment
9. Library Automation; and
10. Visit to Libraries / Information Centres in and around twin cities of Hyderabad and Secunderabad.

For almost two and half decades i.e. from 1989-2012 it was a long journey for ASC-OU for conducting 20 Refresher Courses in LIS (until July 2012). There was a sea change in formulating the Course Contents keeping in view the trends and developments in LIS and especially the emerging Information and Communication Technologies knocking at the doors of LICs and Library and Information Science Schools in the Country. The following topics were included in the 20th Refresher Course in LIS conducted by ASC-OU. These include: LIS present Scenario, Citation Standards, E-books, E-Learning, Preparation of Seminar and Group Projects, IT in Libraries Development, Primary Sources in Libraries, Preparation of MRP proposals, Open Access Movement, Institutional Repositories, Introduction to Nano-Science and Technology, Changing Dimensions of Librarianship, Advances in IRS, Copyright Law, Bibliographic Control in India, Social Networking Technologies, Digital Libraries, Evidence Based Librarianship, Management of Electronic Resources, Hyper Media / Hyper Text / Multimedia, SOUL Library

Automation Package, E-Publishing, Minor Research Project Proposal Evaluation, Web-blogs, Web Designing, SPSS Data Analysis, and Content Management.

Besides the above core topics, lectures were arranged on topics such as: Pranayama (Theory and Practice), Global Environmental Issues and Sustainable Development. In addition, the participants have to present Seminars and Group Projects which will be evaluated by the experts in the field[28].

REFERENCES

1. The Oxford English Dictionary. 2nd Edn. (1989). Oxford, Clarendon Press, 1989. V18. P.372.
2. Antai, A. S. Management of Human Resources. Caliber, Pyramid Publishers, 2002.
3. *http://en.wikipia.org/wiki/main-page. accessed on 10.08.2013.*
4. Saxena, R. S. Importance of Continuing Education for librarians and information scientists. *In* Continuing Education for Librarians. Ed. by J. L. Sardana. Delhi, Indian Library Association, 1984. P.58.
5. ALA Guidelines to the development of human resources in libraries... *Library Trends*, July 1971.P.47.
6. Gopinath, M.A. Identification of areas and programmes for continuing education for libraries in India. *In* Continuing Education for Librarians. Delhi, ILA, 1984. P.32.
7. Stone, E. W. Continuing Library Education. New York, ASIS, 1974. P.30.
8. Sardana, J. L. and Krishna Kumar. Continuing Education for Teachers of LIS: A Systems Approach. *In* Continuing Education for Librarians. Delhi, ILA, 1984. P.27.
9. Houle, Cyril O. The role of Continuing Education in Current Professional development. *ALA Bulletin*, V6, 1961. P.260.
10. Rajan, T. N. Opportunities and Challenges in the Library and Information field....with special reference to continuing education programmes. *In* Perspectives in Library and Information Science. V2. *Ed.* by S.N.Agarwal *etal.* Lucknow,

Print House (India), 1982l. P.92.

11. Guha, B. Continuing Education of Library and Information Specialists. *Lib.Sc.*, V15, N3, 1978. Pp.113-115.
12. Rewadikar, S. Continuing education for teachers of Library Science. *ILA Bulletin*, V15, N 1-2, Jan-June, 1979. Pp.38-46.
13. Gupta, Pawan K. Continuing Education for Librarians and the Library Schools. *In* Continuing Education for Librarians. Delhi, ILA, 1984. Pp.161-164.
14. Rajan, T. N. Opportunities and Challenges in Library and Information Field.... *Opcit.* Pp.89-95.
15. Sudarshan Rao, S. and Vishwa Mohan, V., who have suggested the list of topics.
16. Rajan, Rudra. Continuing Education for Library and Information Professionals in National Library of India: A proposal. *In* LIS Education, Research and Training: Vision 2020. IATLIS 2011. Patiala, DLIS, Panjabi University, 2011. Pp.557-558.
17. *www.universityofhydedrabaddistanceeducation.com.* Accessed on 04.10.2013.
18. Anjaiah, M and Sudarshan Rao, S. Education and Training of LIS professionals in India. *In* Manpower Development for Information Management in Competitive Environment. XIX IATLIS National Seminar (2002) Papers. Hyderabad, IATLIS, 2003. Pp.155-162.
19. National Policy on Education: Programme of Action. Govt. of India. Ministry of Human Resources Development, Dept. of education. New Delhi, 1986.
20. Ibid., P.42.
21. Academic Staff Orientation Programme. New Delhi, UGC, 1987 (Mimeographed).
22. Raju, A. A. N. Planning for Professional Advancement Programmes in Library and Information Science. *Herald of Library Science*, V30, N3-4, July-Octo.1991. Pp.167-174.
23. Raju, A. A. N. Continuing Education Programmes for Teachers in LIS... New Delhi, 58 IFLA Conference, 1992. Booklet 7. Division: Education and Research. Pp.7.3-7.4.
24. *University News.* V51, N2, Jan 14-20, 2013. Pp.15-16.
25. Raju, A. A. N. Planning for Professional Advancement Programmes in LIS. *Opcit.* Pp.167-174.

26. Panganayya, N. B. and Talwar, V. G. Continuing Education of Library professionals and Teachers in LIS. *In* Information and Society. Ed. by L. S. Ramaiah *etal.* New Delhi, Ess Ess Publications, 1997. Pp.143-144.

27. Raju, A. A. N. Planning for Professional Advancement.... *Opcit.* Pp.167-174.

28. UGC Academic Staff College, Osmania University, Hyderabad. 20th Refresher Course (02.07.2012 to 23.07.2012) Programme Sheet.

10

Future of LIS Education, Research and Training in India

LIS education in India marched a long way completing a century. During these hundred years of history it had many ups and downs. In its long journey it trained the required manpower to manage library and information centres established throughout the country especially after India attained independence in1947. The national five year plans gave phillip to the establishment of number of R & D Institutions, higher educational institutions such as Colleges and Universities, Scientific Institutions, National Laboratories in Scientific and Defense fields. The State Governments also took initiatives for the establishment of a network of Public Libraries through library legislation and strengthening school education by establishment of school libraries.

As a consequence of these developments, a number of public, academic, special libraries and information centres have been established. To manage these diverse types of libraries, the required trained manpower had been provided by the LIS Schools established by the Universities in India. At the semi-professional level, Professional Associations at the national and state levels played a prominent role.

The advent of Information and Communication Technologies (ICT), during the later part of the 20th Century added new dimensions to the LIS education in the country and posed new challenges for its survival. In order to meet the new challenges and train the required manpower in the changed scenario, and for its survival in the future it has to address the following burning issues.

10.1. ADMISSION CRITERIA

A LIS Department or School is one of the several departments in the University setup. It cannot function in isolation. The admission criteria or rules must conform to general admission policy of a University. Therefore, LIS Department cannot have different set of admission criteria or rules. In a particular State, the admission rules differ slightly from University to University. They have to conform broadly to State Government Policies of Admission to Higher Education. The Universities have to broadly follow reservation policy of the State Government. In addition, the intake to particular course differs from course to course. This prevents to admit students with aptitude and quality. Sometimes students with mediocrity get admitted to the course. There is also marked difference of language skills among the students. Because of State Policy of giving weightage to regional or State language also adds to the problem of admitting students with aptitude, comprehension, knowledge and skills. This problem is being faced by all the LIS Departments in India.

As there is no uniform admission policy within a State except CET for Medicine, Engineering, Agriculture, Management and Education, there is no question of having a uniform policy at the national levels since education is a state subject under the Constitution. Therefore, the least a LIS Department can do under the Indian situation is to conduct entrance test for admission to LIS courses. Many Universities in the country have been conducting entrance tests for admission to various courses. LIS is no exception in this regard. Admission tests for LIS courses to certain extent help admitting students with aptitude, knowledge, interest and motivation. The existing admission criteria for LIS courses in the country needs to be streamlined so as to admit better students and in turn, turn out of quality products to meet the present and future needs of employment market in the country.

10.2. LIS CURRICULUM

LIS curriculum is the backbone to turn out well trained manpower. In the past many Committees have been appointed by the University Grants Commission (UGC), India to suggest model curriculum for LIS course so as to maintain certain minimum standards in the light of changes taking place in LIS education and produce quality products.

In this regard mention may be made of curriculum committees appointed primarily by the UGC to bringing out required changes according to fast changing needs of employment market. An elaborate presentation was given in Chapter: E: Committees on Curriculum Development. These include: 1. Ranganathan's Committee on University and College Libraries (1957)[1], Report of the University Grants Commission (UG) Review Committee (1965)[2], 3. UGC Panel on Library and Information Science (1981)[3], 4. Report of the Curriculum Development Committee on LIS (1990)[4], and the latest being, 5. UGC Model Curriculum: Library and Information Science (1998)[5]. This Committee is also known as Prof. C. R. Karisiddappa Committee. It is more than a decade now, no serious thought was given by the authorities at the helm of affairs to appoint another Committee "to take stock of LIS education in India and the wide gap to know its current status and future course of action for its sustenance in the Country".

In addition to the efforts of University Grants Commission (UGC) in this regard, professional associations in the country took initiative and discussed the status of LIS curriculum in the yearly national conferences / seminars. Particular mention may be made of IATLIS and its efforts in bringing out required changes in LIS curriculum so as to meet the present and future requirement of LIS education in the country. The IATLIS Conferences held at Patiala (2006)[6], Dharwad (2007)[7], Pune (21010)[8], and Ahmedabad (2011)[9] strongly advocated "To revise the Curriculum and also bring out a Vision Document on LIS Education 2020 in India".

The advent of ICT impacted every branch of study including LIS education in the country. There was a pressing need to educate and train the required manpower with a strong base on ICT. The trained manpower should meet the present and future needs equipped with sustainable professional competencies. The emerging areas of ICT must find a place in LIS curriculum so that LIS education will have better future. Areas such as digital libraries, open access, information literacy, and managing e-resources must find a place in curriculum of LIS. The LIS curriculum should give thought to very necessary requirements such as: Knowledge of real library work environment, practical knowledge of library automation software and network environment, internet search strategies, communication and soft skills, developing leadership qualities to manage LICs efficiently and effectively, passon towards LIS profession and imbibing professional ethics and service motto.

To have bright future for LIS education in the country, there is an urgent need to bring out a model curriculum for LIS taking into its fold newly emerging areas in ICT and related fields and also issues pertaining to diversification of LIS education to provide new and more avenues for employment.

10.3. INFRASTRUCTURE

Infrastructure facilities in LIS Departments are one of the basic requirements for turning out quality products. Many studies have been conducted to assess the infrastructure facilities available in LIS Departments. The studies revealed, with exception to few departments, that in many departments the situation is very pathetic. In such a situation one cannot expect to impart all that is relevant to the students.

It was stated that since the publication of CDC Report in 2001 in some LIS Departments the facilities of I.T. Laboratories have been improved with exception to Internet Facility. This conclusion is based on the data collected in 1999-2000. With the implementation of ICT in University Libraries, it also enabled the LIS Departments to access such facilities. In such Departments where I.T. laboratories have been established and now being maintained by LIS Teachers. But it is difficult for LIS teachers who are busy with teaching and research to manage I.T. Laboratories efficiently. Therefore, it has been suggested that an

I.T. Technician exclusively to be made available to the Departments to administer the Lab efficiently. Efforts should be made in such Departments where I.T. Lab facilities are lacking at present, to install such facilities at the earliest. Otherwise they may lag behind in imparting the practical training and experience in I.T. and turning out well trained manpower to meet the diverse needs of employing agencies.

10.4. STAFF STRENGTH

It is a fact that many LIS Departments in the Country presently suffer from insufficient staff strength, which in turn hinders to impart quality teaching to the students. This leads to overburdening of teachers in teaching and neglecting research and publication activity. In the past, committees have suggested staffing pattern for LIS Departments. Ranganathan Committee on University and Colleges Libraries[10] appointed in 1957 in its report published by the UGC in 1965 stated that Teacher and Student Ratio should be 1 to 10 in the B.Lib.Sc Course and 1 to 5 in the M.Lib.Sc Course.

The Report of UGC Review Committee[11] appointed in 1965 and headed by Dr. S. R. Ranganathan "to review the standards of teaching and research in Library Science in the Universities" published under the title *Library Science in Indian Universities* (1965) recommended, under the sub-heading 10: Staff Requirements that "a staff-student ratio of 1:10 at B.Lib.Sc level and of 1:5 at the M.Lib.Sc level as reasonable. Here staff means full-time staff. In our view, a Department of Library Science conducting the B.Lib.Sc Course should have a minimum staff of one Reader and two Lecturers and a Department conducting M.Lib.Sc, Course should have a minimum staff consisting of one Professor, two Readers and four Lecturers. The old practice of employing the University Library Staff as part-time teachers should be discontinued as early as possible".

The Panel on Library and Information Science appointed by the UGC[12] at its meeting held on September 19, 1981 in its recommendations under the heading 'Faculty' recommended that "A Department conducting both B.Lib.Sc., and M.Lib.Sc. / M.L.I.Sc Courses and with more than 40 students in each class respectively, requires the following full time teaching staff:

i.	Professor	1
ii.	Readers	2
iii.	Lecturers..	5

In the case the number of students exceeds 15 in the M.Lib.Sc. / M.L.I.Sc., Class, the provision should be for *one additional teacher for every 5 students* or fraction thereof..... In case a Department plans to offer M.Phil, andPh.D. programmes, the additional staff requirement should be calculated keeping in view various factors such as nature of courses, specialization, number of options to be offered etc".

The Working Group (WG) on Libraries appointed by the National Knowledge Commission[13] recommended under Appendix 10: Staffing pattern and staff requirement of libraries (P.28) at recommendation V: Staffing Patterns of LIS Departments (P.32) and at sub-recommendations 2-4 stated "that the minimum staffing pattern for B.L.I.Sc, Course should be as follows:

I.	Professor	1
II.	Reader	1
III.	Lecturers	2

The minimum staffing pattern for MLISc Course shall be as follows:

I.	Professor	1
II.	Readers	2
III.	Lecturers	4

There should be a 1 : 10 student-teacher ratio".

In the past, studies have been under taken and recently by Prof. Paramjeet Kaur Walia, Prof. R. S. R. Varalakshmi, Prof. Pijushkanti Panigrahi to assess the present position of LIS education in the Country. Prof. Walia[14] studied LIS education in North India, which include among other things infrastructure including staff strength of the LIS Schools in North India. Prof. Varalakshmi[15] surveyed LIS education in South India. She provided figures pertaining faculty and infrastructure. Prof. Panigrahi[16] studied the present state of LIS education in East and North East India. He provided figures for human resources (Faculty) and infrastructure (traditional and IT Tools).

The above cited studies present not so a rosy picture of LIS education. Especially most of Departments, with exception to few and those under Central Universities, are under staffed and the infrastructure is not on the expected lines. In most of LIS Departments established under State Universities this type of situation is prevailing. This affects quality of LIS education. No less a person than the President of India Shri Pranab Mukherjee while delivering Convocation address to the 45th Convocation of Utkal University, Bhubaneswar held on April 25, 2013 stated that "shortage of faculty is major hindrance for delivering quality education in our Universities. The standard of education cannot be allowed to suffer due to this constraint. Filling up of vacancies must therefore be given high priority"[17]. In the light of this concern expressed the President of India, State Governments should support the State Universities for filling up of vacancies existing in various faculties including LIS Departments.

10.5. LIS RESEARCH

In Chapter 7 LIS Research India, an elaborate treatment has been given to this aspect. More than eighty LIS Departments offer research courses leading to the award of M.Phil and Ph.D. degrees. The quality of LIS Research has been the subject of critical study and evaluation. M. P. Satija[18] in his thought provoking paper titled "What Ails Doctoral Research in Library and Information Science in India?", critically discussed the various facets of LIS Research in India and asks five questions to measure the worth of the research work. These include:

i. How many papers based on the research have been published in referred and international journals?

ii. How many dissertations have been published as independent and readable book?

iii. How many times such a research work has been quoted or cited in text books or other derivative works or collateral research?

iv. It would too much to ask if any patent has been granted on the research work.

Another burning problem faced by the LIS research in India, especially for admissions to M.Phil and Ph.D. programmes is unhealthy admission policies pursued by LIS Schools. These admission policies were not able to attract committed, suitable and motivated research scholars to pursue research and produce quality research products. The reservation policies of universities even in admission to research courses, perhaps, may be one of the reasons for not admitting meritorious candidates for research courses. The result is 'substandard' research output.

Non availability of required research supervisors / guides is another burning problem in some of the LIS Departments. In some of the LIS Departments the Research Supervisors were burdened with more number of research candidates. As the research supervisors are burdened with teaching and other departmental activities, they were not able to spare required time to guide their scholars. Lack of expertise on the part of research supervisors to guide the students on the research areas selected by them, especially in the emerging areas of Information and Communication Technologies (ICTs), perhaps, may be another reason resulting substandard research output.

Another unhealthy trend noticeable in LIS Research in India is 'give and take' policy of awarding M.Phil and Ph.D. degrees. In majority of the cases 'favourable reports' are secured from the external examiners. In some cases the Research Scholar was asked to resubmit the thesis incorporating the issues raised by the external examiners. In very few cases the thesis is rejected or thorough revision is needed. On the whole the entire process is 'stage managed'. This unhealthy trend undermines the quality of LIS research.

The need of the hour, if we want to raise the standards of LIS research is to strengthen the LIS Departments with sufficient staff and infrastructure and scrupulously following the ethics of librarianship and adhering to personal ethics by the Research Supervisors / Guides.

Another facet of LIS Research in India is award of Emeritus Fellowships / Professorships by the University Grants Commission for retired teachers. In addition, it also awards major / minor research projects to the teachers in the Universities. Retired teachers also can avail this facility. These awards are bestowed on the applicants who submit research proposals for study and investigation. Many retired teachers in LIS have been awarded emeritus fellowship / professorships for a period of two years.

After the end of the two years, the awardee has to submit his / her research report to the UGC through proper channel. Before bestowing the award, the research proposal is referred to the expert(s) for evaluation. On the recommendations of expert(s), the fellowship is awarded. But after submission of the research report, it is not evaluated by the UGC. The 'research reports' lie in the offices of the UGC. In the case of major / minor research projects, the applicants are being called to the UGC Office at New Delhi to present their research proposals before an expert committee. The award of major / minor research projects depends upon the recommendations of the so called expert committee. Indian Council for Social Science Research (ICSSR), New Delhi also awards Senior/Junior Research Fellowship to the teaching community including retired teachers.

The research reports submitted by LIS teachers, including retired teachers, to the awarding agencies like UGC and ICSSR, for example, have not seen the light of the day. With exceptions to few research reports on various aspects of LIS, majority of them have not been published. Is it not sheer wastage of academic exercise? If they are published, the image of LIS Department will be enhanced and add to the research output.

10.6. IMPACT OF ICT

It has been recognized by one and all the impact of ICT on the lives of the people all over the world. Every subject field had been impacted by ICT and Library and Information Science is no exception. The technology has transformed and brought revolutionary changes in the information world in every aspect, its organization, processing and accessibility and the careers of our outgoing graduates are also on the whirlpool of this transformation. The impact of ICT has changed the traditional methods of information management and delivery system of information. Therefore there is greater responsibility for LIS Schools in India to turn out well trained manpower in ICT and this needs revamping of LIS Courses and required changes have to brought into LIS Curriculum. This is a new challenge thrown against the LIS Schools. It is now evident that these "Profound changes in the information world with the influence of ICT demands similar levels of changes in the pattern of education and make the products of the schools suitable for work in the ever expanding information environment". There is no future for such LIS Schools which lag behind in adopting ICT to turnout quality products.

10.7. ACCREDITATION OF LIS PROGRAMMES

The University Grants Commission (UGC) established National Assessment and Accreditation Council (NAAC) in the year 1994 at Bangalore with a mandate "to assess and accredit Higher Education Institutions in India and with an objective of maintenance and improvement of quality in Higher Education". NAAC has been very actively engaged in the performance evaluation and implementation of quality sustenance procedure in Universities and

Colleges in India[19]. The NAAC does not assess individual Courses but higher educational institutions as a whole. Therefore the question of accrediting individual Courses / Departments does not arise.

In USA, the American Library Association (ALA) does the work of accrediting library schools. In UK, the Council of National Academic Awards is the body which takes care of accrediting LIS Schools. But in our Country the Library Associations were not in a position to take up the job of accrediting LIS Schools. They are not in a position to show professional leadership and struggling hard for their survival. IATLIS at its National Seminars discussed the issue of accrediting LIS Schools. IATLIS at its 22nd National Conference held from 24-26 November, 2005 held at Trichy discussed the issue under the main theme "Quality Education in Library and Information Science". The Conference inter alia recommended that:

a) The NAAC should take immediate measures for develop norms for accreditation of LIS programmes to ensure quality education and training.

b) It is also recommended that the UGC, AICTE, NAAC and DEC have to appoint an Expert Committee to develop a set of quality norms / standards and ensure their implementation uniformly in all LIS Departments in India".

As it is, the Universities in India are autonomous bodies and they may not like the courses offered by them have to be accredited by professional organizations like ILA, IASLIC and IATLIS. The appropriate body is NAAC which has been equipped with necessary mechanism, wherewhittal and expertise. It has issued guidelines and indicators for the academic libraries to provide quality library and information services to their user community. Accreditation brand add value to the LIS Courses.

10.8. GLOBALIZATION OF LIS EDUCATION

In the era of globalization, LIS education in the country should gear itself to compete with best LIS Schools in the World. To achieve this, the LIS Schools should be equipped with required staff strength, quality infrastructure and updated syllabus incorporating latest developments in Library and Information Science field. Quality LIS education will attract foreign students especially from developing countries like Africa, South and South East Asia and also from Latin America. Already in some of LIS Schools in India foreign students are being admitted to pursue LIS Courses of their choice and in few cases research courses like M.Phil and Ph.D, programmes. This in turn will enable the Universities to earn precious foreign exchange and strengthen the financial position of Universities in India. LIS Schools cannot ignore this trend any more. Already few LIS Schools in India have been attracting foreign students for study and research.

10.9. PLACEMENT AND EMPLOYMENT COUNSELING

During the past three and half decades, trained library professionals with ICT background had better employment opportunities. This is because of establishment of various types of libraries especially academic, technical, special and industrial libraries. This trend is due to globalization and liberalization policies pursued by the Government of India. Those trained professionals with good exposure to Internet, WWW, E-resources, and Digital Libraries have better chance of employment opportunities. LIS Departments in the country should establish 'placement and employment counseling Cells' so as to market their products. 'Forming Alumni Associations' also will go a long way to help the outgoing students to get better employment opportunities. As it is, very few LIS Departments have 'placement and guidance cells' as is the case with management, Computer Science and Engineering Colleges, which ha been effectively assisting the outgoing students for securing better job opportunities. Placement and Counseling Services will ease the unemployment problem to certain extent and in turn the LIS Schools will have better future.

Continuing Education Programmes (CEP) can also be undertaken by the LIS Departments to the raw professionals and those who were working so as to enable them for professional up gradation. This will enable the working professionals to get career advancement in the parent organization or join new institutions in better positions. The LIS Department should think of conducting 'employable Courses'. The Departments can also think of adopting 'finishing school concept' in the form of supplementary / add on courses. Such add on courses allow students to transform unemployable to employable work force. If possible online courses may be conducted by select LIS Departments having infrastructure facilities and required well trained staff and of course support from the concerned University Authorities. CEP has been discussed in detail in Chapter-9: Training of LIS Professionals. The CEP may generate some revenue which help LIS Departments to strengthen existing infrastructure facilities.

10.10. COLLABORATION

In many Universities LIS Departments are working in isolation without collaborating with the sister departments in the concerned faculties such as: Social Sciences, Arts, Sciences, Engineering and Technology and Management. For example LIS Departments can collaborate with Departments such as: Management, Computer Sciences, Statistics, Psychology and Economics and so on to design and offer new courses with the expertise and resources available in these better off departments.

The National Knowledge Commission (NKC) in one of its important recommendations emphasized the need for collaboration and participation with public and private partnership. This collaboration for example would be between 'Publishing houses, information industry and LIS Schools'. LIS Schools also can collaborate with publishing industry both print and electronic to expand the scope for LIS professionals 'with their background knowledge on content and structure of information sources and services and to enable them to project their importance to the prospective and potential customers.

Another important area which the LIS Schools can think is of offering Consultancy Services. The schools can offer their expertise to the newly established Library and Information Centres (LICs) to organize their collections both print and non-print and introducing computer based information services. LIS Schools can also offer consultancy to especially School Libraries, mostly Government School Libraries which are in bad shape in almost all the states of India. Organizing the library collections on scientific lines in the old and famous libraries having very rich and valuable collections is another important area for LIS schools to stepin and to offer expertise for rejuvenation of heritage libraries. This consultancy, if undertaken can generate some revenue to LIS Schools.

In the foregoing paras of this Chapter an attempt has been made to identify certain crucial areas of far reaching consequences and importance to LIS Departments in India. The future of LIS education in the country very much hinges upon these identified areas and the LIS Departments are expected surmount these obstacles which may come in their march towards better future. Let us hope that LIS education in the Country will have better future in the years to come.

(*Note*: This Chapter is based on the inputs provided by Prof. C. R. Karisiddappa, Prof. R. S. R. Varalakshmi and Prof. V. Vishwa Mohan).

REFERENCES

1. *University and College Libraries.* New Delhi, UGC, 1964. P.228.
2. *Library Science in Indian Universities: Report of the UGC Review Committee,* New Delhi, UGC, 1965. P.86.
3. Guidelines for BLISc / MLISc Courses. Prepared by UGC Panel on Library and Information Science, New Delhi, UGC, 1982 (Mimeographed).
4. *Report of the Curriculum Development Centre in Library and Information Science.* New Delhi, UGC, 1992. P.157.
5. *UGC Model Curriculum: Library and Information Science.* New Delhi, UGC, 2001. P.147.
6. IATLIS. 23rd National Conference. 23-25 November, 2006 held at DLISc, Panjab University, Patiala. (Recommendations).
7. IATLIS, 24th National Conference, 19-21 November 2007 held at DLISc, Karnatak University, Dharwad. (Recommendations).
8. IATLIS, 27th National Conference. 2010. DLISc, University of Pune, Pune. (Recommendations).
9. IATLIS, 28th National Conference, 26-28 November, 2011 held at Gujarat University, Ahmedabad. (Recommendations).
10. *University and College Libraries. Opcit.*

11. *Library Science in Indian Universities. Opcit.*
12. Guidelines for BLISc / MLISc Courses... *Opcit.*
13. *Libraries: Gateways to Knowledge: A Road map for revitalization.* New Delhi, National Knowledge Commission, 2007.
14. Walia, Paramjeet Kaur. Library and Information Science Education in North India. *DJLIT.* V30, N5, September 2010. Pp.9-18.
15. Varalakshmi, R. S. R. LIS Education in South India: Perspective and Challenges. *DJLIT.* V30, N5, September 2010.Pp.19-31.
16. Panigrahi, P. LIS Education in East and North East India: Retrospect and Prospect. *DJLIT.* V30, N5, September, 2010. Pp.32-47.
17. *University News.* V51, N33, August 19-25, 2013. P.28.
18. Satija, M.P. What Ails Doctoral Research in Library and Information Science in India. *DJLIT,* V30, N5, September 2010. Pp.61-66.
19. Hegde, Ganesh. National Assessment and Accreditation Council and its relevance to RUSA. *University News,* V51, N39, September 30-October 06, 2013. P.148.

Index